The Library of Orthodox Theology

No. 3

RUSSIAN PIETY

The Library of Orthodox Theology

Published under the direction of
B. Bobrinskoy, O. Clément, B. Fize, J. Meyendorff
and N. Struve

RUSSIAN PIETY

BY

NICHOLAS ARSENIEV

TRANSLATED BY ASHELEIGH MOORHOUSE

THE FAITH PRESS
Wing Road, Leighton Buzzard, Beds. LU7 7NQ

St. Vladimir's Seminary Press
New York

FIRST PUBLISHED IN ENGLISH IN 1964

This translation © Asheleigh Moorhouse, 1964

Translated from the French
(Editions Delachaux et Niestlé Neuchâtel and Paris)

Second Edition 1975

PRINTED IN GREAT BRITAIN
in 11pt. Garamond type
BY THE FAITH PRESS LTD
LEIGHTON BUZZARD

SBN 7164 0314 5

CONTENTS

INTRODUCTION

THE world to-day is passing through a critical period. It has been driven into a corner: before it yawns the abyss of total physical destruction, brought on by its own internal disintegration. This abyss only serves to reveal an abyss more terrifying still, one which affects not only the physical existence of mankind but also his spiritual life. The whole history of man has always been a great conscious or unconscious search for God. If this hidden thread is broken, what will become of the cultural, moral and spiritual life of mankind?

Although this question confronts all nations and all men, it confronts above all the Russian people. This is due in the first place to the leading role played by Russian Communism in the atheistic movement of our time. It is also due to the fact that the Russian people, although they are no better than others, have shown themselves rich in religious possibilities, in the past as also now. It is this religious experience which has, throughout the centuries, shaped what has been best in the character of the people. In particular the great Russian literature of the nineteenth century would be incomprehensible if it were not for the hidden, nourishing presence of this spiritual sap.

* * *

Russia, or rather her present leadership, has been trying ostentatiously to march on other paths. Everything has been done to ban the 'ghost' of religion, although this has proved to be a more lively ghost than was expected.

The broad lines of the persecution of religion by the Soviet régime are well known. Christians by the hundreds of thousands have suffered for their faith, have been executed, imprisoned, locked up in concentration camps, where many have died of hunger, epidemics, ill-treatment, torture. The 'cloud of witnesses' —'witnesses to the point of blood'—has become immense in Soviet Russia.[1] It is hard to imagine the cruelties perpetrated in cold

---

[1] Some very vivid details concerning the confessors and martyrs of the faith in Soviet Russia are provided, for example, in the remarkable works of Andrey Russinov (Evgeny Gagarin), *Die grosse Tauschung,* Breslau, 1936, and *Auf der Suche nach Russland,* 1938, and Alexandra Anzerova (Anne Arseniev), *Aus dem Lande der Stummen,* Paderborn, 1936. These books are based on personal memories of great value.

7

blood by butchers who want to destroy their victims not only bodily but also in the soul. The butchers are often cheated, however. The prisons become places for an apostolate *in vinculis:* priests and bishops who have been imprisoned with thieves and murderers have converted more than one criminal. . . . It is impossible to estimate the number of victims who perished for being faithful and active Christians. Innumerable churches were plundered and closed, works of sacred art, furnishings of the church, Eucharistic chalices, ancient icons, religious books were profaned or destroyed in a kind of rage, or, in the first years after the Revolution, were sold abroad for next to nothing. On the eve of the Second World War there were whole regions, like the province of Orel, where only a single church remained open in a radius of four or five hundred kilometres. In Archangel, a city of importance which at one time had more than thirty churches, only the cemetery chapel remained open. In the southern part of the province of Leningrad not one church was open when the Germans arrived. In Moscow, of the 600 churches which existed before the Revolution only twenty-three remained, and these examples could be multiplied indefinitely.

In some of the deconsecrated churches 'anti-religious museums' were set up, full of caricatures and obscene and blasphemous inscriptions. Up to 1936 the clergy were deprived of all civil rights, even the right to remain in the cities and work—something which doomed them to die of hunger. Priests were hunted down like animals. They could not conduct services or administer the Sacraments without a government authorization (which very few succeeded in obtaining), and this authorization applied only to the particular church in which the priest was serving. Any infraction was punished by deportation to the 'death camps.'

But it was especially the soul which the Soviet régime wanted to condition. Beginning at a very early age, in the schools, they tried to defile the imaginations of children with coarse and sacrilegious images. All religious instruction up to the age of eighteen, even within the family, was forbidden under penalty of deportation. The State encouraged informers. Children were invited to denounce their parents when the latter continued to observe religious practices. Occasionally children did make such denunciations. The Church was barely tolerated, as a group of cultic associations, and the cult was limited to a small number of sanctuaries spared by the State. Wounded in the body of her faithful members, especially the clergy, and without any official system of education, the Church was gagged, and seemed to be losing all influence in the life of the people. She seemed doomed to extermination.[2] And yet she was not exterminated. On the contrary, the census of 1937 showed that the number of believers was much greater than the Communists had thought, and above all it proved that a great number of Russians were not afraid to bear witness to their faith before the authorities.

The Second World War brought a sudden change in this situation. At the most critical moment for the Soviet State the Metropolitan Sergius turned to the faithful and exhorted them to defend their native land against the invader. The Church's moral support was a tremendous help to the State in its fight against the Germans, and the State was not ungrateful. Some degree of existence was permitted to the Church, a considerable number of churches were restored as places of worship (the Germans had already done this in the territory they occupied, something which could not fail to influence the decision of the Soviet government), and the Church was able to open eight seminaries and two theological academies to candidates for the priesthood. A kind of *modus*

---

[2] The following works contain concrete information presented in a systematic way: (1) *Das Notbuch der russichen Christenheit*, N. Arseniev, Fritz Lieb and Hans Koch, 1930 (cf. my article); (2) *Christenverfolgungen in Sowjet-Russland*, Siegmund-Schultze, Gothe, Klotz, 1930 (cf. my two articles on pp. 17 and 41); (3) *Welt vor dem Abgrund*, I. Ilyn, Eckart-Verlag, Berlin, 1932 (cf. my article); (4) my article, *Die russische Kirche hinter dem Schleier*, Hochland, Munich, September 1936, pp. 512–25; (5) my article, *Die gegenwartige Lage der Religion in Sowjet-Russland*, Hockland, 1938; (6) my article, *Religious situation in Soviet Russia*, World Dominion, London, January 1938, pp. 10–22; (7) the German book of Konrad Algermissen on religious persecutions in Russia; (8) P. B. Anderson, *People, State and Church in Modern Russia*, New York, 1949; (9) *New Russian Martyrs* (in Russian), by Archpr. M. Polsky, Jordanville, N.Y., 1949; (10) Archpr. D. V. Konstantinov, *Orthodox Youth in the Struggle for the Church in the U.S.S.R.* (in Russian), Munich, 1951; (11) Prof. A. A. Bogolepov, *The Church under Communist Domination* (in Russian), Munich, 1958; (12) *Religion in the U.S.S.R.*, Munich, 1960 (published by the Institute for the Study of the U.S.S.R.); (13) Alexander Kishcowsky, *Die Sowjetische Religionspolitik und die russische orthodoxe Kirche*, Munich, 1960 and especially Nikita Struve, *Les Chrétiens en U.S.S.R.*, Paris, Editions du Seuil, 1963, p. 357; cf. also the excellent and ample reports in *Irenikon*, *Russie et chrétienté*, *Istina*.

vivendi was established between the Church and State, the hierarchical structure of the Church was recognized by the State, which in fact put the Church under its authoritarian and watchful tutelage. The Church was made a cog in the machinery of a totalitarian State, and above all a means of propaganda abroad. Henceforth the danger for the Church, a very grave danger, was on the moral level.

High ecclesiastical dignitaries have indeed made speeches full of flattery toward those in power, full of statements which unfortunately have not corresponded with the facts. Many articles of this type have appeared in the official journal of the Moscow Patriarchate.

The danger that the Church might be internally corrupted through the offices of some of her leaders was counterbalanced, however, by a fact of the utmost importance: *the freedom of liturgical prayer, the freedom of public worship.* This freedom was not absolute, but it was nevertheless much greater than in the more difficult times of persecution. This was a freedom of prayer and not very much beyond that, except of course an education for future priests, and the official recognition of the hierarchy, albeit fettered and exploited. But after all this freedom to pray in public gatherings and the increasingly frequent participation in the Eucharistic Communion represent a great fact: it is here that transcendent forces converge, are concentrated—and *influence* life. Here is where the source of spiritual renewal wells up.[3] This life and this spiritual thirst have a power which surpass all calculation. Here, in these *depths* of the spiritual life, the atheistic dimension of Communism is perhaps already conquered.

This is why the Communist authorities have recently decided again to alter their attitude toward the Church—in the face of this purely *religious* threat (since for many years now Christians have been loyal citizens of the Soviet State). A new persecution has descended upon Russia, not a bloody one, it is true, but one that is suffocating, aimed especially at preventing the development of a Christian *way of thinking.* More than 7,000 churches have been

---

[3] For several years now the Soviet authorities have been trying by all sorts of pressure, and recently even by force, to prevent the attendance of young people and children in church.

closed in the past four years. Two seminaries have been closed (at Kiev and Stavropol) and two others are on the way to being closed, out of the eight which have been in existence since 1946. Several bishops—among them the most energetic in the field of evangelism—have been deprived of their dioceses, deported or imprisoned (for example, Bishop Michael of Smolensk, exiled to the Urals, and Archbishop Job of Kazan, condemned to three years in prison). Harassment of the Church and her believers is increasing. The ideological campaign against religion is once more raging and is often accompanied by oppressive administrative measures. By a number of violent measures the authorities are now destroying the celebrated monastery of Pochaev, centre for a number of pilgrimages in south-west Russia, and most of the monks have been deported. Children are now by decisions of Soviet courts torn away from parents believing in God and placed in children's homes.

．　　．　　．

The religious events that take place in Russia have a significance which goes beyond the borders of Russia. The faith which lives in great sections of the Russian people, and which to a large extent has been rekindled, purified and strengthened by the example and intercession of hundreds of thousands of martyrs, is fighting against the most systematic and aggressive atheism of modern times. This atheism endeavours to found itself on the data of science, wrongly, of course, since contemporary science, far from leading to atheism, leaves us on the threshold of an infinity or mystery which it is just barely able to glimpse. This aspect of present day physics is dismissed and ignored in Soviet Russia; at least officially, for among the new *intelligentsia* many seem to look for other solutions. Instead, the immense technical advances, the 'conquest of interplanetary space,' the possibilities of thermo-nuclear energy are touted as proofs of the unlimited quasi-divine potentialities of the man of the future, and are utilized systematically by the theoreticians and preachers of atheism. All these facts, presented with fatuous certainty and without the slightest critical spirit, can appear convincing to simple and primitive minds (their whole argument is indeed fundamentally naïve). But now, in spite of this scientific influence and the very widespread existence of an atheism which is often simply conformity, faith still exists, is propagated, and possesses arguments untouched by atheistic propaganda; it is not only on the defensive; it is also speaking to the heart, and revealing to it *the reality and presence of God.* Sometimes it takes hold of the best of the younger generation. It is Christian faith which inspired Pasternak's religious poetry and philosophical and historical meditations, and made them echo so loudly in the hearts of Russian young people; it is faith which fills the churches; it is the same power which—still unconsciously—is awakening in youthful hearts a nostalgia for spiritual values, for a deeper personal existence that is irreducible to Marxist patterns, to technical materialism. *Nostalgia for God* (often unconscious) and *faith in God* : here are the two streams which are converging in a hidden way in modern Russia. If these tendencies were not gaining ground it would be impossible to understand the uneasiness of the Soviet leadership and the attacks on religion. which have been renewed since 1958, and especially since the end of 1960.

Many Russians are being again drawn to the eternal springs by which the people have been nurtured for centuries, despite their imperfections, faults and weaknesses. It is from these sources that they have drawn their most noble and creative inspirations. The spiritual destiny of Russia depends on the renewal and deepening of these contacts.

. . .

To explore—or at least to suggest by a series of soundings— the depths of the religious life of a people is an arduous but exciting task. Especially if it deals with a people whose history, at this very moment, embraces and sums up the spiritual drama of mankind.

Two fundamental elements must be distinguished in our subject : on the one hand the features of national psychology, on the other hand the very substance of the faith. What is decisive—whether we are speaking of the experience of a nation or of an individual —is the second element, for the revelation of the living God is the pivot of history for the Christian. The data of 'natural' psychology —among other things, national psychology—are secondary and subordinate from the Christian viewpoint, no matter how instruc-

INTRODUCTION

tive and significant they may be. Nevertheless, it is very interesting to study the interaction of these two elements. The Christian will see here the action of grace on nature, the purification and growth of natural phenomena under the rays of grace, and also, sometimes, he will see the dangers which can come from the impress of a national character on the Christian way of life, the imperfections and deformations which can ensue.

Above all we will find joy and comfort in contemplating for a little while some of the summits of Christian sanctity, a sanctity in which the luminous peace of Christ shines brightly and which, while it never changes in its depths and ultimate inspiration, is gloriously refracted in the rich and concrete diversity of history.

NICHOLAS ARSENIEV

Sea Cliff, New York
December 24, 1963

CHAPTER ONE

THE NOSTALGIA FOR SPACE AND THE CONTRASTS OF THE RUSSIAN SOUL

THE nostalgia for space, the far-distant reaches of vast, unlimited space, can be regarded as one of the most conspicuous features of the psychology of the Russian people. This has been said many times, occasionally in an oversimplified and exaggerated way. Nevertheless, just as the 'force of the earth' has been aptly identified, by the Russian writer Gleb Uspensky, as a force which subjugates the soul of the peasant, so too, in a larger sense, has the 'force of space' influenced the Russian mind, without any distinctions as to social or cultural origins. In the long run the Russian suffocates in the over-urbanized atmosphere of central and western Europe, with its crowded cities, its over-civilized country-side, and the narrow horizons of its landscape. This nostalgia for open space has played an often decisive role in the historical life of the Russian people; many of the positive and negative features of her history and culture may be explained by it at least in part. The colonizers of the huge 'Eurasian' plain, the adventurers (*ushkuyniki*) of the republic of Novgorod who went down the great rivers of northern Russia, pillaged the people along the way and founded military and commercial bases in the name of their mother republic and to the glory of 'St. Sofia of Novgorod'; the Cossacks who plunged into the depths of central and eastern Siberia and even crossed the Bering Straits to settle on the American continent; the peasants who, in search of work, staked out the great highways of European Russia; and finally the stream of pilgrims which moved back and forth across the whole breadth of the land, leading sometimes to the 'saints of Kiev' in the famous Kiev Crypt Monastery, sometimes to the 'Wonder-working saints of Solovky' on the islands of the White Sea in the far north, sometimes to one of the many monasteries in the Moscow region, for example, the monastery of Trinity St. Sergius—all these travellers, adventurers, brigands, explorers, seekers of employment, pilgrims and colonists manifest with more or less intensity the nomadic element which plays its part in the psychology of the Russian people.

The poetry of space is often revealed in popular songs, in those melodies so full of nostalgia and life, and it has left its mark on the soul and work of many poets and artists. Here is Koltsov's *The Reaper*, who mows with a youthful zest in the midst of an immense carpet of grass, in the boundless solitude of the Voronezh steppes. . . .

> Stretch forth, my arm,
> Cut wide and well, my hand,
> Come, noonday wind,
> And blow upon my face!

When he had finished his two great epics *War and Peace* and *Anna Karenina*, Leo Tolstoy was in the summer of 1879 considering the writing of a third epic work, in which he wanted to represent the Russian people as a force of peaceful expansion, attracted by great open spaces. During this period of his life he loved to go out on to the highway leading from Moscow to Kiev, which passed very close to his country home, and to talk there with those countless people going along the road on foot, especially with the pilgrims coming that way from the most distant places in Russia, from Orenburg and Siberia, to visit the relics of the saints and the famous churches of Kiev.[1] He called these his 'excursions into the great world.'[2]

Let us linger for a while with these pilgrims. A religious feeling had developed among them about which we will have occasion to speak more than once. A certain nostalgia of a spiritual nature reveals itself here, drawing these believers, who were often suffering and disturbed souls, to the places where evangelical fervour had burst forth in the past, and where it continued to shine even now . . . especially to wherever a *starets* was still to be found, one of those men of God full of the spirit of discernment and the power of uninterrupted prayer. Eighty years ago the Russian ethnographer, S. Maximoff described the feelings of some pilgrims

---

[1] cf. the *Private Journal* of Leo Tolstoy, March 9th, 1879.
[2] cf. *Literaturnoe nasledstvo* (Literary Heritage), edited by the Russian Academy of Sciences, Vols. 37–8, 1939, pp. 104–6.

when they suddenly viewed the long-awaited panorama of one of these 'strongholds' of the Lord. 'Behind the little grove of aspens,' he wrote, 'a lofty hill is suddenly visible. On its summit the many crosses of the monastery churches are blazing in the sun; the pilgrims could count seven churches. Two bell towers rose from among them—one slim and straight, the other squat and dumpy, cut off at the fourth story. The main cathedral, dedicated to our Saviour, could be seen with its five cupolas, and the church with the saint's tomb, built like a tent out of stone, with its one cupola painted blue and decorated with gilded stars. A white stone wall went round the monastery as far as the eye could see, running down the slope of the hill, clinging to the out-croppings of rock, half embedded in the foliage of a dense wood. At the sight of this view which opened suddenly before them in all its marvellous beauty, the crowd of pilgrims fell to their knees and began to murmur prayers. Sighs were audible, and exclamations, and some-times sobs, interrupting the words of prayers asking for the inter-cession of the holy Abbot, of the Most Holy Queen of Heaven, the Holy Mother of Kazan, or of Tikvin, or the Holy Mother of "The Burning Bush," as they call her.' [3]

The 'Holy Mountains' (*Svyatye gory*) to the south of Russia, the monastery of Balaam with its many hermitages on the austere islands of the huge lake Lagoda, the monastery of St. Seraphim of Sarov in the forests of Nizhni Novgorod, the famous hermitage of Optino where the great *startsi* of the nineteenth and the begin-ning of the twentieth century have shone so brightly, the monas-tery of St. Mitrophan of Voronezh, and that of Zadonsk with the relics of St. Tikhon, who lived in the eighteenth century, the monasteries in the region of Moscow, St. Savva of Zvenigorod, the New Jerusalem monastery on its beautiful site, the monastic centres of the north country in the forests of Vologda and Arch-angel, on the shores of lakes and rivers—such as the famous monastery of St. Cyril of Belo-ozero, and other monasteries scattered as far as Siberia (e.g. the monastery of Irkutsk with the relics of St. Innocent, the missionary bishop)—combined with the three main centres of the Lavra of St. Sergius, the Crypts of Kiev and the Islands of Solovetsky—all these exercised a tremendous

[3] S. Maximov, *Wandering Russia* (in Russian), St. Petersburg, 1877, pp. 243-4.

influence on the soul of the Russian people. Sometimes buffeted to extremes, full of burning faith, this troubled soul would find in these places the peace and spiritual comfort which it needed. In this way a kind of 'aesthetic of pilgrimage' evolved: the joyous transfiguration of nature and the wandering life through a spiritual experience and at the same time by a naïve freshness of impression, and a certain spirit of adventure. This was an aesthetic transcription of the dynamic quality so characteristic of the Russian people. The aged Daryushka was a simple old village woman who had at an early age fulfilled all her family obligations toward her orphaned younger brothers and sisters, and had dedicated herself to a life of charity, prayer and pilgrimage. She has described the joy she felt on her first departure from home, the delights of this journey on foot across the infinite expanses of fields, prairies and forests, surrounded by a nature restored to life. Her description is that of an aesthetic ecstasy, deeply penetrated by religious feeling: 'When we left our village and looked about us—Lord, it seemed to us that God's world had no end or limit. What divine grace shines on high in the heavenly places! And down here underfoot, here is the green grass, and the golden corn; and over there is the forest, almost too thick, you'd think, to pass through. When you walk in silence, or rest on the ground, you think you are hearing a constant chanting, full of gentleness. Everything is humming and gurgling, dripping and murmuring around you, as if the Lord Himself were speaking to you through the mouth of all creation!' [4]

One of the heroes of Turgenev's *A Sportsman's Notebook,* a strange little old man full of tenderness and poetry, the peasant Kasyan, a veritable child of nature, who knows all the plants and animals of the forest, although he is normally a timid person with a wild look and taciturn, weighed down by silent wisdom, suddenly speaks of the beauty and violent joy of wandering across the great open lands: 'Why, what's to be done, then? Really, you can't sit at home for ever, can you? So when you set out . . . when you set out . . .' and here, becoming excited, he suddenly raised his voice, '. . . then you begin to feel better, you really do! And

[4] From the review *Domashnyaya Beseda,* St. Petersburg, 1864.

the sun shines down on you, and God has a better look at you, and when you sing, the notes come more easily. Here's some grass growing; so you look at it, and notice it. The birds of heaven sing. . . . And over there, beyond Kursk, the steppes begin. Ah! Those steppes! How wonderful, there is pleasure for a man! There you can breathe freely, there is something that's a real gift of God! And they stretch out, so they say, even to the warm sea, where lives the Gamayun bird with the sweet voice, where the leaves never fall either in winter or autumn, where golden apples grow on silver branches and where every man lives in joy and righteousness . . . that's where I'd like to go. . . . Oh, I've been around a good bit already. I've been to Romny, I've been to the famous city of Simbirsk and even to Moscow, with its golden cupolas. I've been on the banks of our life-giver the Oka, and on the gentle river Tsna, and on our mother Volga. . . . And many another peasant in bast shoes has wandered over the world looking for Truth too. . . . That's so. What is there to stay at home for, eh? There's no righteousness in man, and that's the truth . . .'

A searching for the peace and spiritual nourishment which will satisfy the soul thirsting for righteousness—here is an outstanding feature of many of these pilgrimages, trips and wanderings. Sometimes it takes on the quality of a kind of popular 'romanticism.' Thus the Old Believers dreamed of a country where true faith and righteousness would reign, beyond the forests and wastelands, far away in the Orient. This was the 'Kingdom of White Waters' located on a hundred isles. There were even mysterious itineraries copied by hand and circulating among the Old Believers since the eighteenth century, which described in detail the complicated and difficult road which had to be taken.

'After passing all sorts of cities, rivers and villages, you come to the village of Ustba, where there is a chapel. In this village you must go to a certain Peter Kirillov, who will be ready to provide you with lodging and will show you the road that leads on from there. At first there are snowy mountains to cross. On the other side of the mountains there is the village of Damas, also with a chapel; near this chapel lives the holy monk John. You must go to see him. Beyond that there is a forty day journey on foot across the Kigisse country and another four days of walking to the Tatania, and then you have arrived.'[5] According to other legends of the Old Believers the country of true faith and social justice is at the bottom of the miraculous lake of Kitezh, in the Volga forests. There it was that the holy Prince George II, with all his possessions, his family, his troops and pious subjects, was delivered by a miracle of God, at the time of the cruel Tartar invasion, so that the true faith might be preserved. And even up to to-day you can enter into relations with this wondrous people of Kitezh. In the silence of the night you can hear, if you lie down in the forest near the water, with your ear to the ground, the ringing of bells rising up from the depths of the lake, and you can sometimes see light. Once a boy disappeared. And yet he did not die, for his parents received a letter from him in which he told them that he was still alive, and that it was not necessary to pray for him as if he were dead. 'I am in a terrestrial kingdom, in the invisible city of Kitezh, with the holy fathers, on an island of beauty and peace. Believe me my dear parents, this terrestrial kingdom is a place of peace, of quietness, of joy and gladness. Around me the holy fathers are flourishing like the lilies of the vale, like palms and cypresses. Out of their mouths a continual prayer rises to our heavenly Father. When night falls this prayer can even be seen: it rises toward heaven like a pillar of fire and a bursting shower of sparks; and when this happens you can read and write as if by the light of a candle.'[6]

A social and moral revolt against the injustice that reigns on earth sometimes went hand in hand with these dreams. This revolt found a radical expression in the strange and rather small sect of 'Fugitives' (*beguny*) who appeared here and there all over northern Russia, especially in the eighteenth and in the first half of the nineteenth centuries. These 'fugitives' left their families and homes, renounced all forms of ordered life, and flaunted their refusal to accept any form of authority, which they regarded as an emanation of the Anti-Christ. They refused to submit to any form of census or to take out passports, and took refuge in the forests. The nostalgia for the desert life is again encountered in the rather primitive and mediocre rhymed verses which they loved to sing,

[5] cf. Vladimir Anderson, *The Old Believers and Sectarians* (in Russian), St. Petersburg, 1900, pp. 174–5.
[6] cf. the article by the ethnographer Prishvin, 'Before the Walls of the Invisible City,' in the review *Russkaya Mysl*, January–February, 1909.

a nostalgia for the immense forests 'where the cuckoo sings in the trees of the wilderness,' for the vast plains 'where the rivers flow at God's command.'

This nostalgia for space, this love for roaming and travel, fed by the spirit of curiosity and restiveness, also took hold of many people in the more cultured circles of Russia. But in this case it led rather to the West, and long before the Revolution and the emigration which followed it a great many Russians—whether they were representatives of the old aristocracy or proponents of revolutionary ideas (at times, of course, these two elements would paradoxically coincide)—were transformed into men without a real home of their own, into 'seekers after the Absolute' (Gogol, Chaadayev, Nicolas Stankevich), into seekers of Truth and Righteousness in all parts of the world. They sought to quench their spiritual thirst or satisfy their hunger for novelty and adventure, and sometimes to indulge their lack of moral balance and uninhibited radicalism, in the ancient cultural and spiritual traditions of Europe, in the main streams of Western religious, philosophical and aesthetic thought or, again, in the profusion of new social and revolutionary ideas (one thinks here of Herzen and Bakunin, among others). One of the most typical representatives of this attitude in Russian literature (but without the revolutionary and destructive element) is Versilov in Dostoevsky's *A Raw Youth,* a seeker after the Absolute and certainly unstable and impassioned, but with a noble heart and a thirst for Truth.

• • •

These deep stirrings are not simply expressions of a lust for travel. There is here also an element of anguish and spiritual quest. For very often in the Russian psyche there is not only an *immoderate element,* but also, at the same time, *a passionate nostalgia for moral balance and spiritual peace.* The Russian soul often lives in contradictions. The two poles which exist in every nation and every individual sometimes exist in the Russian soul in almost immediate proximity, and are perhaps for this reason more evident, more accentuated. Dostoevsky sensed these latent contradictions vividly. As pictures of everyday existence in Russia his representations of Russian life and psychology are of course quite inadequate, one-sided and exaggerated. There is his often morbid predilection for everything hysterical and eccentric; if the majority of Russians were as hysterical as most of Dostoevsky's heroes, no normal life could ever be established there! What Dostoevsky does, really, is to dig down into the depths, showing us the hidden places, the *potentialities* of the Russian soul, lying beyond empirical life. And here he excels, often possessing a kind of clairvoyance—a cruel insight, as it has been rightly observed, but also saturated with the burning love that he had for his people, and his concern for their spiritual salvation. We are familiar with Dostoevsky's famous psychological essay, in *The Diary of a Writer*, where he shows us the Russian soul bending over the abyss, and suddenly overtaken by a moral vertigo. On the one hand, he tells us, an imperious instinct drives Russians to excess. With hearts pounding they draw near the precipice, with a desire to lean half way out over it and to plunge their gaze to the bottom of the pit, and even, in some cases (which are by no means infrequent), to fling themselves into it like madmen. On the other hand, 'when the individual Russian (or the entire nation) has gone to the very limit and it is impossible to go further,' then, says Dostoevsky, 'the thirst for repentance and salvation awakens in him, with the same violent force.' And Dostoevsky feels that the urge to repent and recover one's moral health is more serious and goes even deeper than the urge to negate and commit spiritual suicide.[7]

This psychological breadth, filled with spiritual promise and at the same time with spiritual danger, is manifested in many outstanding personalities who may be regarded as representatives of both the defects and the positive characteristics of the popular mind. I am thinking in the first place of that 'Magnificent Prince of Taurida,' Potemkin, not the creator of those 'Potemkin villages' as his detractors are accustomed to say, but the creator of a whole great new country—a 'New Russia'—along the coast of the Black Sea. He tore whole provinces out of the wilderness and integrated them into civilized life. An indefatigable worker, he had grandiose and even fantastic schemes, but at the same time he involved himself in the most concrete details of colonization. He almost quadrupled the population of these provinces in nine years, founding the cities of Nicolaev, Kherson, Ekaterinoslav, Simferopol,

[7] cf. the essay 'Vlass' in *The Diary of a Writer*, 1877.

Sebastopol, Nakhichevan, Mariupol, Stavropol and many other urban centres. He attracted colonists from every country, built up a proud navy—the Russian navy of the Black Sea. He erected churches, monasteries, ports, shipyards, fortresses, barracks, hospitals, factories, schools, the latter in three languages—Russian, Tartar and modern Greek—to meet the needs of the people, and had textbooks printed in these three languages. He reformed the army throughout the Russian Empire, taking the greatest pains to better the lot of common soldiers, whom he loved, as he said, 'like his own children,' and to establish a more humane and effective discipline. At the same time he fostered measures of religious toleration throughout the Empire, which he applied especially to the colonists who had come at his invitation to settle the vast provinces he administered in the south of Russia, provinces which had been (as with the Crimea) acquired by Russia at least partly as a result of his diplomatic genius. This man of unlimited energy was hurrying to consolidate Russian power in the Black Sea area before the outbreak of a new war with Turkey. He once slept only three nights during a sixteen day trip by sled from the coast of the Black Sea to St. Petersburg, almost the whole length of Russia. For the rest of the time, during the night, he dictated an almost unbroken stream of notes and orders to his secretaries and assistants, who had to be constantly relieved, while during the day he made inspections, visited churches and received the deputations of local authorities. But a man of such an active and dynamic nature must also have moments of profound physical and nervous lassitude. He would rest for days at a time half sitting up on a Turkish sofa, unshaved, clad only in his dressing gown, and yet even in this relaxed state and in spite of this external indolence, he continued to give orders, and to keep an eye on the course of public affairs, all the while receiving generals, ambassadors and ministers. Sometimes, however, attacks of profound melancholy, an overwhelming *taedium vitae,* would deprive him of all desire to enjoy life and work. For it must be said—if we are to become aware of all his contradictions—that this violent worker was also a violent pleasure-seeker. He loved women and courted them assiduously, he loved luxury, precious stones, objects of art, and knew how to acquire them. He loved to construct palaces, pavilions in the oriental fashion, with slim moresque columns hung with brocades and silks. He made the preliminary sketches for these projects himself. He loved gardens. He arranged enchanting parties, lavishly provided, such as the one he gave for Catherine II (who was in all probability his legal wife) in 1791 in his Tauric Palace at St. Petersburg, in an effort to get back into her favour. This party was a fairyland of gems, lights, fountains, exotic plants and animals, marble statues and gold decorations. How can this extravagance be reconciled with the constructive genius of a great man of State, this irresponsibility in the use of money with the responsibility he felt more keenly than most generals of his time for the life and well-being of his soldiers? Especially his attacks of sadness, the boundless disenchantment which would suddenly invade his soul, his disgust for life and its pleasures and even for the most useful and productive activities, the sense of the vanity of everything . . . all of this was an outright contradiction of the other aspects of his life. Nor was this sadness merely the glut of a man who has feasted on the pleasures of life and is sated with honour and glory, with well-being and voluptuousness. This sadness had also a metaphysical origin. In fact, among the papers kept after his death by his nephew, Count A. I. Samoylov, the following 'Poem of Contrition' (*Pokayanny kanon*) was found, addressed to our Lord Jesus Christ, written in his own hand, and composed by him in the last years of his life, probably at his headquarters in Yassy.

'As we incur Thy righteous wrath, O God, every hour of our lives, how is it that we do not fear Thy judgment, and do not see ourselves as worthy of eternal punishment? But the depths of Thy mercy cannot be measured. . . .

'I have recourse only to a pure contrition, O Lord, as I commit myself to Thy mercy. . . . I have become a slave of sin and have defiled the robe of my salvation, and do not dare to raise my eyes to heaven. Thou art merciful; hear me, O Lord.[8]

'Behold my humility, O Lord, behold my repentance. Purification and salvation are found only with Thee. Have pity on Thy unworthy creature, and let not my soul perish. . . .

[8] This passage was certainly influenced by the celebrated 'Penitential Canon' of St. Andrew of Crete (seventh century), which is recited in Orthodox Churches during the first and fifth week of Lent.

'O Lord, behold Thy creature, who is nothing but dust before Thee. My soul is afflicted. Judge me, O my Saviour. I have sinned before Thee, as a man; but I have not lifted up arms to another God. Thou only art righteous and holy. . . .

'O my soul, behold thy Saviour before thee, who has redeemed thee by His blood. Thou seest His wounds. This is the Lamb of God, who bears the sins of the world. . . .

'I am afraid, O Lord, to invite Thee into the temple of my soul. But because I know how gracious Thou art toward sinners, I open my heart and soul before Thee, and beg Thee, like the centurion in the Gospel, to speak one word only that I may be saved.

'Behold, Thou hast measured my days a span long, and my whole being is as nothing before Thee, O Lord. In this world my life is subject to suffering and anguish, and in the world to come I only know that I shall be rewarded according to my works. . . .

'O Lord, hear my prayer, and let my cry come unto Thee. Turn not Thy face from me. Thou hast known my waywardness and frailty. To Thee alone is my heart open. Thou seest my contrition. Behold now, Thy creature cries out to Thee. I pray that Thou wilt save me. Do not forget me, unworthy as I am, but remember me in Thy kingdom. Have pity on me, O God, have pity on me!

'I lift up my hands to Thee, O my God. I adore Thee, my Creator, with a contrite heart and a pure conscience. I believe and I confess that Thou art my Saviour, and I truly wait for my salvation at the hands of Thy mercy. I commit my soul and body unto Thee. Spare me, O Lord, through the intercession of Thy saints. It is to Thee only that I address my prayer. Hear me, O Lord!' [9]

Torn by contradictions, this man's troubled soul found its anchor of salvation in this prayer.

There is another soul torn by contradictions—not unlike that of Potemkin : it is the soul of Leo Tolstoy. This tremendous genius, this great artist, full of vitality and a vast overflowing strength, is a realist . . . but a realist illumined by the vision of Beauty, *a realist passionately in love with the beauty of life.* He roots himself deeply in the soil, in order to draw nourishment from this vast life which presses in on him from every side; he feels himself

[9] Published among the papers of Potemkin in the review *Russian Archives,* Moscow, 1881, II, pp. 17–18.

carried along by its streams, he deeply loves its great eddying currents, the great cycles continually being renewed—the cycle of family life, the annual cycle of nature, the cycle of work upon the land. He is enraptured by the beauty of family tradition, and knows how to depict it for us with compelling charm, as in his great epics *War and Peace* and *Anna Karenina,* and in his delightful novel *Family Happiness.* The poetry of childhood and adolescence, the great life which opens up before young people on all sides, full of promises and unknown horizons, the first virginal love of youth, the poetry of courtship, the education of the first children, the gentle, familiar intimacy of parents and children, the image of the mother—all these things go to make up the fundamental tissue of life, and all shine with the glow of beauty. The old customs and traditions of ancient families, especially those living in the country. Winter nights, with the moon lighting up the vast expanse of snow, and the track of sleds over the broad, silvery plain. The morning hunt in summer, when the dew moistens Levin's high boots as he plunges into the thick grass. The nights of August, in the old park, fantastic and enchanted, with the moonlight transforming everything, making things more distinct, putting them in a strange relief and instilling in them a new life, transfigured and mysterious . . .

But this same Tolstoy is gripped violently by the sense of nothingness, instability, a gulf in which all things are swallowed up, all beauty, all that we possess, all that we love, all that we are. Consider the cry of Tolstoy's soul in his famous *Confession.* In the midst of the greatest family happiness, in the most favourable external circumstances, recognized and pampered as a literary genius in Russia and western Europe, in full possession of his marvellous talent, at the summit of his literary achievement—he suddenly feels the approach of something strange which he calls 'the arresting of life.' The meaning of life is gone. Terrible questions rise before him: 'Why do anything? Well, and after you have done it, then what?' There is no answer. 'My life came to a standstill,' writes Tolstoy. 'I felt that the foundation on which I had been standing had fallen away, that I had nothing left to hold on to, that what I had been living by no longer existed, that I no longer had any reason to live. . . .' The abyss had opened before his eyes. The abyss engulfing all things. And the whole second half of his life is a search for answers to these questions. The solutions which develop in the mind of Leo Tolstoy are theoretical and abstract, they do not have the force of his terrible feeling of the impending void. They are less alive than the burning experience recorded by Dostoevsky; the experience of salvation by way of the Cross, of God's unbounded condescension, even to the very depths of our helplessness and misery. But Tolstoy's search, a hunger not satisfied even up to his death, the inner restlessness which made him leave his home at the age of 83, secretly, on a dark November night, to go in search of peace for his troubled soul, all this can be considered as characteristic of a Russian soul, still deeply dissatisfied even when it has reached the summit of its natural achievements.

I shall not dwell any longer on the contradictions (at times so painful) in the soul of the Russian people. I will simply repeat that such oppositions are common to all men, to all nations. But this conflict is often set in sharper relief, and seems to be more unexpected and more violent in the psychology which we are studying. This is what makes the religious psychology of the Russian people so very interesting, not just from the ethnographical viewpoint, but from the point of view of man in general, and above all from the religious point of view, for here grace is operating on disputed ground.

CHAPTER TWO

THE ORTHODOX CHURCH: HER LITURGICAL, CONTEMPLATIVE AND SACRAMENTAL LIFE; HER MORAL AND ASCETICAL TEACHING

THE popular Russian soul, with its disquiet, its instability and its excessive emotional faculty, found its balance and the backbone it needed so much in the Christian message, in the creative and regenerating power of the 'Good News,' and the life stemming from it. The Good News came to the Russian soul by way of the Orthodox Church. And this raises a very interesting question: How may the piety of this Church be characterized? (I am not speaking here of the abuses and human imperfections of its members, which are to be found everywhere, but of the very essence of this piety.) What are its essential characteristics, its vital centre, the fundamenal inspiration of its life?

It may be said that what is decisive in the Orthodox Church is the *contemplation of the glory of the Incarnate Word;* a truly 'Johannine' contemplation, for the whole character of this Church, taken at the highest levels of her spirituality, is profoundly 'Johannine' (not excluding, however, an equally profound 'Pauline' element). Unceasing contemplation—full of trembling and love— of the mystery of our Lord's unbounded condescension: of His Incarnation, His Cross, and of the glory, the victorious, transfiguring power of His Resurrection! These two poles—the divine *Word,* that is made *flesh*—are both present in the spirit of the Church in a way that is peculiarly Johannine. Through this historic, concrete, vivid and palpable reality ('that which we have seen with our eyes, which we have touched with our hands'); through this truly lived existence so full of humility and sacrifice; through these genuine sufferings . . . there is disclosed a 'metaphysical' background or depth of divinity which dazzles the captivated eye. 'I see a strange and glorious mystery: here is a cave, like heaven, and a Virgin, who is the throne of the cherubim, and a manger, containing that One whom the whole universe cannot contain . . .

These are the words of a Christmas hymn; and there are also, especially, the hymns (or visions) of Holy Week:

'To-day He who suspended the earth upon the waters is Himself suspended on the Cross. The King of Angels is crowned with thorns; He who clothes the heavens with clouds is Himself clothed in a mantle of shame. He who set Adam free in Jordan is now struck in the face. He who is the Bridegroom of the Church is nailed to the Cross. The Son of the Virgin is pierced by a spear. We worship Thy sufferings, O Christ. Show us also Thy glorious Resurrection.

'When Thou wast nailed to the Cross, O Christ, all creation trembled at the sight. The foundations of the earth shook, stars fell and the veil of the Temple was rent. The mountains tottered, the crags were split asunder. And the good thief called out, with us: "O my Saviour, remember me when Thou comest into Thy Kingdom." '

The theme which keeps returning constantly between man and God in the one person of Christ: this Man who suffers, nailed to the Cross, is the Creator of both heaven and earth.

'To-day the Lord of all creation appears before Pilate, the Creator of all things is delivered to the Cross. By His own will He allows Himself to be led like a lamb; He is fastened by nails; His side is pierced; He who made the Manna rain from the skies is refreshed with a sponge; the Redeemer of the world is humiliated; the Creator of all things is struck by His creatures. O such mighty love for mankind! He prays for those who crucify Him to the Father, saying: Father, forgive them, for these sinful men do not know the evil that they do' (Vespers for Holy Saturday).

The immense condescension of the Divine Majesty, His coming down to us in the abyss of our sin and helplessness, this essence of the whole message of the Gospel constitutes also the central experience of the Eastern Church (and of all Christianity, to the extent that it remains faithful to the primitive message), and has deeply touched the heart of the Russian people. This central theme of the Christian faith has deeply impressed itself upon them, in spite of all their imperfections and sins. This intense emotional contemplation of the boundless compassion of their Saviour has led and still leads the Russian people, in spite of all hostile propaganda, to crowd the churches during the moving services of Holy Week. I am thinking especially of the night between Friday and Holy Saturday, when the Saviour's burial is commemorated and a linen cloth is set out in the middle of the church—the 'shroud' representing Christ lying in the tomb. Funeral chants are sung or read, expressing the mystery of the divine condescension, alternating with verses taken from Psalm 119 (or 118 in the Eastern Church):

'Blessed are those who live without reproach, who walk in the way of the Lord.

'Thou who art Life hast descended into the tomb, O Christ; and the angelic hosts were overcome with dread as they glorified Thy condescension.

'Blessed are those who keep His testimonies; who seek Him with their whole heart.

'O Life, how can it be that Thou hast died? How couldst Thou go down into the grave? But Thou hast destroyed the kingdom of death and dost deliver the departed from the depths of hell.

'Those who walk in His ways commit no evil.

'We glorify Thee, Jesus our King, and we venerate Thy burial and the sufferings by which Thou hast saved us from corruption.

'Thou hast ordained that Thy commandments be followed diligently.

'It is Thou who hast established the measures of the earth, and now Thou art laid in a narrow tomb. O Jesus, King of the universe, Thou hast now raised the dead from their tombs.

'O that my life might be according to Thy commandments in every way.

'O Jesus my Christ, Lord of all things, what wert Thou seeking when Thou didst descend to those in hell? Was this too the redemption of mankind?

'I will not be confounded, for I have respect for all Thy commandments.

'The Lord of the universe is revealed as dead, and is laid in a new tomb; He who emptied the tombs of their dead.

'I bless Thee from a pure heart, for Thou teachest me the righteousness of Thy judgments.

'O Life, Thou hast descended into the tomb, and by Thy death, O Christ, Thou hast destroyed death, and hast caused life to spring forth for the world.'

What is especially characteristic of the Eastern Church, then, is the feeling of *the victorious irruption of Eternal Life* accomplished in the Resurrection. The triumph of eternal life is already here revealed in the flesh. This is baffling, incomprehensible, it runs counter to all the possibilities and all the 'laws' of nature, and it is precisely this which is our salvation. It is certainly this inspiration of the primitive message which breathes in the Paschal joy of the Orthodox Church. The emphasis on resurrection is thoroughly apostolic. There is no Good News, there is no salvation without the Resurrection of our Lord. 'If Christ is not risen from the dead, then all our preaching is vain, and your faith is vain. . . . But Christ is raised from the dead, the firstborn of the dead' (1 Cor. 15 : 17, 20). It could be said, in fact, that the whole Good News and our whole salvation is concentrated in the fact that Christ is raised from the dead. Without the Resurrection the Cross is only a defeat. In the Resurrection God gives striking proof that He is the Lord of the universe. Here is the answer to our anxious expectations. Here, in the Resurrection, we already have an anticipation of our own victory over death, of the ultimate victory of eternal life. But this ultimate victory is not only a hope, it has been won already in the victory of Christ. Eternal life has already entered into the world, in a hidden way of course—and yet it has been manifested in the Resurrection of Christ. It is a much more substantial reality than ours, it is the divine reality, the reality of eternal life, which has entered our reality and our life by the decisive fact of the Resurrection. This ardent and joyful faith, this Paschal exultation, permeates the entire religious attitude of the Orthodox Church, her experience, her doctrine, her prayer. There is here a profoundly personal and at the same time corporate emphasis, and still more, a profoundly cosmic emphasis, involving the salvation of all creation. The victory over death, already realized in Christ, concerns *the whole of creation*, it is the central and decisive fact in the history of the whole world, the decisive turning point in its destiny. A new era began then with the victory of Christ, even if this era has still a hidden quality. All the forces of evil which still reign in the world, death, suffering, wickedness, are in principle already deposed, already put to shame, already destroyed and crushed in this victory. This is why all creation is invited to participate in the joy of Easter. A cry of triumph; the joy of the emancipation and restoration of creation, of our reunion with God, of our rehabilitation to and participation in eternal life, a joy that takes possession of one's whole being, body and soul; the trembling adoration of this fullness of life which has entered into the tissue of our existence and has vanquished death . . . such are the themes of the Church's hymns on the night of Easter. Behold Christ coming out of the tomb, like a Bridegroom shining forth from the wedding chamber. Here is the Sun of righteousness, the giver of life, rising from the grave. It is the inexhaustible source of life eternal which gushes out of the rock of the tomb—more truly life-giving than that other spring, its imperfect figure, which Moses made to flow out of the dry rock in the wilderness. 'Let the heavens rejoice, let the earth be filled with gladness, let the whole world visible and invisible celebrate this day, for Christ is risen from the dead, eternal joy!' 'All things are now filled with light, heaven, and earth, and even hell. Let all creation celebrate Christ's Resurrection, which is its life.' 'To-day all creation dwells in joy and gladness, for Christ is risen from the dead and hell is overcome.' 'We celebrate the death of death, the destruction of hell and the beginning of new life—of eternal life.' 'A Holy Easter has appeared to us to-day, a new and Holy Easter, a mystical Easter, a sacred Easter! An Easter which is Christ our liberation! An immaculate Easter, the great Easter, the Easter of the faithful; the Easter which opens the doors of paradise and sanctifies all the faithful!' 'This is the day of the Resurrection, let us be illumined with joy, let us embrace one another and address each other as brothers! Even to those who hate us let us say: Let us forgive one another for the sake of the Resurrection, and let us sing: Christ is risen from the dead. He has triumphed over death by death, and has given life to those who were in the tombs.'

Here is the heart and core of the Christian message. Here is the shining centre of the life and piety of the Orthodox Church. And the soul of the Russian people, even the simplest among the people, has been profoundly influenced and shaken by this Paschal joy.

* * *

The cosmic character of the Good News, that rehabilitation of creation which is celebrated by the Paschal Feast and arises out of the fact of the Saviour's Incarnation, Cross and Resurrection, does not enter our life in an external or 'magical' way. On the contrary, it is indissolubly united with the crucifixion of the 'old man,' with a life of moral tension and effort, with the regenerating and sancti- fying action of the Holy Spirit. The Church exhorts us to untiring effort and an unceasing moral combat. The chief enemy is the 'I' of self, the 'old man.' We ought to have no pity on him, we ought to crucify him and mortify him in his proud self-sufficiency. We are called to a purification not only of our external actions but of our whole spiritual life, of the very roots and most hidden corners of our moral being. We must constantly fight against the thoughts of sin which assail us from all sides. 'The purification of the heart —that is perfection!' cried St. Macarius of Egypt. There is a quality of virility, courage and spiritual sobriety that penetrates this teaching and experience.

'This is the will of the Spirit,' writes Isaac of Syria, 'to those in whom He dwells He does not teach indolence, but just the opposite. The Spirit urges them not to seek repose, but to devote themselves to work and great sufferings. Through temptations the Spirit strengthens them and leads them to acquire wisdom. This is the will of the Spirit: that His Well-beloved perseveres in the struggle.' 'If the soul has not consciously tasted sufferings for the love of Christ, it cannot yet be united with Christ.'

We are like a fortress besieged on all sides, we are God's soldiers. Here is one aspect of the Church's teaching, in which the accent is on the virile qualities of the soul, on the elements of activity, tension and effort.

But we do not save ourselves by our own powers. This is com- pletely excluded, for we are weak, unstable and powerless. The impossibility of salvation by our own efforts is therefore set forth with the same urgency. This is the other side, no less evident, of the same basic experience. 'The human spirit is not in a position to resist the temptations of demons by its own power. It should never even attempt to do this.' These are the words of Hesychius of Jerusalem (fifth century), and other ascetical and mystical fathers of the Eastern Church say the same thing again and again. There is a dilemma here: We are called to be soldiers of God, we are called to virility, courage and activity, to effort and spiritual combat, and yet we are feeble, powerless, and ought not even to dare to enter into the fray on our own resources. How may we resolve the dilemma? This is, of course, St. Paul's experience. There is only one way: the constant invocation of Jesus, and prayer addressed to our Saviour, and the cry of the heart in distress; He it is then who comes to our aid and fights for us. The same Hesychius continues, in the passage just quoted: 'But if you invoke the name of Jesus, they (the spiritual adversaries or demons) will be unable to resist you even for an instant, or to do anything to you whatever.' 'It is impossible,' he goes on, 'to purify the heart of evil thoughts without the invocation of the name of Jesus.' 'When you call upon Jesus,' writes Philotheus of Sinai (about the beginning of the ninth century), 'He easily consumes all that is tainted with sin. For nothing can be our salvation, other than Jesus Christ. It was He Himself, in fact, who said this.' This solution to the dilemma is indeed very Pauline, grounded in the New Testament, and thoroughly Christocentric. We are weak, but in Christ we become strong. The solution therefore lies in constant prayer, in the untiring invocation of Jesus. We are called to be active, but we cannot be active by our own power. For it is He who comes to fight for us and to sustain our efforts. Grace and effort go hand in hand, therefore, in this life which comes from Christ Jesus. There are the gifts of the Spirit, the grace of perseverance in combat, the virility of the soul, spiritual heroism, the process of sanctification and ascension which begins *now* and to which we are called *now*. But all these are *gifts*, powers which He lends to us and which He can withdraw at any moment. Nothing really belongs to us. Hence the *humility* that is always present in real sanctity.

This humility is not a 'virtue' that is added, it is the fundamental quality of the holy soul who sees himself in the presence of God, who sees his own littleness and feebleness, and God's greatness.

This humility is constantly, persistently and forcefully inculcated in all the moral and spiritual teaching of the Eastern Church. It is this humility—together with gentleness, simplicity, kindness, and a spirit of restraint and spiritual equilibrium—that shines with such radiance on the faces of the desert fathers, and in the personalities of the great saints and righteous men of the Russian Church.

There are a number of written texts which reflect this humility. The abbot Dorotheus (sixth–seventh century), whose homilies have been regarded by the Eastern Church as one of the best introductions to the spiritual life, provides us with a whole philosophy of humility. He compares human souls with fruit trees. When trees bear much fruit the branches bend down toward the ground under the weight; in contrast, the branches without fruit stand up straight and high. There are even trees whose branches are weighted down with rocks in order to force them to bend and bear fruit. The same thing happens with souls: when they humble themselves they become rich in fruit, and the richer they become the more they humble themselves. This is why the nearer the saints approach God the more they see themselves as sinners. Thus Abraham, when he saw God, called himself 'earth and dust,' and Isaiah, when he beheld God throned in majesty, cried out 'Woe is me, a man of impurity!' [1]

And here are some accounts—or rather, incidents—from the lives of the desert fathers, which characterize this spiritual attitude. St. Anthony leaves his cell in the morning and sees the whole world covered with the snares of the Demon. He is terrified. 'Who then can be saved?' he cries out to God. And the divine voice answers: 'The humble one. And I tell you more: these snares will not even touch him.' The same St. Anthony once prayed to God that He would show him someone who was better than he, who could serve as his example. He told Anthony to go to Alexandria; the first man that he met at the entrance to the city would be the one God had sent in answer to his prayer. Indeed he did meet a man at the entrance to the city, and questioned him.

---

[1] Philocalia (selections from the ascetical and mystical writings of the Orthodox Church, containing texts from the fourth to the fourteenth centuries), Russian trans., Vol. II, p. 648.

Who are you? I am a tanner. And what do you do? I am busy at my tannery and serve my customers. But what are your works before God, your forms of self-denial? I have none. But what do you do then? How do you spend your day? I spend my day working. And what do you do then? How do you serve God? Describe your day to me. Well, in the morning, after I get up, I place myself for several moments before the face of God, and I think that in this whole great city of Alexandria there can be no one who is as great a sinner as I. And in the evening, before going to bed, I again place myself for a few moments before the face of God, and again I think that in all this great city of Alexandria there is no one who is as great a sinner as I. Such was the lesson God sent to St. Anthony.[2]

Or there is the holy abbot Siso, on his death-bed after a long life full of struggle, interior combat, and the fruits of sanctity. The anchorites who were his neighbours and disciples have come to take leave of him. As he nears his end his face is illumined, and he cries out to those who are gathered round him: 'Behold, the abbot Anthony is coming!' And his face shines more and more, and he sees the various orders of saints in glory approach his bed in turn. Suddenly he is heard to speak to someone. And the elders ask him: 'To whom are you speaking, Father?' And he replies to them: 'The angels have come to take me, and I am begging them to leave me here a little longer, that I may repent.' And the elders say to him then: 'But you have no need to repent, Father.' He answers: 'I tell you truly, I have not even begun to repent.' And they saw then that he had attained perfection.[3] For 'What is perfection?' Isaac of Syria once asked. And his reply was: 'The depth of humility.'[4]

There is another element which should be distinguished in this teaching, ideal, or experience of sanctity, and that is: *spiritual sobriety;* the tone of humble virility, full of spiritual discernment combined with child-like, gentle and benign simplicity, a simplicity that already belongs to the highest level of sanctity and touches on the sublime.

---

[2] I have put this incident into my own words, and have developed the dialogue to some extent. An account of it may be found in *Apophtegmata Patrum.*

[3] P.G. 65, col. 396.

[4] *Homily* 78.

The soldier of God must be manly, and this manliness must be humble and sober. The ascetical and mystical fathers emphasize and highly value this sobriety of the soul as the fundamental or *true* attitude, the very essence of the new life. 'Spiritual sobriety,' writes Hesychius of Jerusalem, 'is the pathway of all virtues, and of divine command. It is also called silence of the heart, and it is the same thing as vigilance of the spirit—a spirit which has attained the state of perfect non-dissipation of thought.'

This spiritual sobriety, that goes hand in hand with vigilance of the heart, this gentle circumspection, humble and virile, nourished by a life of constant and untiring prayer, manifests itself also in a great distrust of all religious emotionalism, all exaggerated or hysterical emotional expression, a distrust of all over-emphasis on the uncontrolled affective element in the spiritual life. It is also revealed in a hostility toward the intrusion in one's life of any element of sensuality, however it may be concealed or disguised, in a general distrust of sensual imaginings—in short, a hostility toward the indulgence of any excessive religious fantasy, toward the spiritual attitude which would give free reign to visions and ecstasies.

Gregory the Sinaite (fourteenth century) writes on this same subject: 'Friend of God, be vigilant and circumspect. If in your spiritual labour you see a light or a fire within you, an image of Christ, for example, or an angel, or of some other being—do not accept it, refuse to accept it, that your soul may not suffer injury.' Fantasy should not be allowed to run wild, the fascination of visual appearances should be resisted. 'When it seems to you that your spirit is drawn to the heights by an invisible power, do not give credence to it, do not let your mind be drawn, but force yourself to work.' In so far as the vision can still be doubted and resisted, it comes not from God, but from the Evil One. What comes from God comes suddenly, in an unexpected and irresistible fashion. 'Often you may think that this is a spiritual joy, when it is only a sensual experience inspired by the Enemy; but those who have spiritual experience will know how to distinguish between the two.' [5]

Once again the *austerity* and the virility of this teaching should

[5] *Philocalia*, Russian trans., Vol. V, pp. 252–3.

be emphasized. The crucifixion of the 'I'—as we have already said —is its main theme. It is the constant struggle with thoughts of sin —'the invisible combat'—an untiring spiritual conflict, and prayer, above all prayer. The whole of this combat and activity is prayer; this whole form of life is prayer. All power comes from prayer, or rather from the One who is called to help in prayer and who comes to deliver us from our enemies and fight for us. And so this whole activity, however manly, intense and courageous it may be, stems from grace, is nourished by grace, is empty and powerless apart from grace. In the austere circumstances of combat and crucifixion there is the presence of the One who comes to our aid—of our Lord Jesus, the Son of God. The austerity of the Cross is also the serenity of the Cross and the joy that flows from it.

．　　．　　．

The joy of the Cross. The joy and sanctification and transfiguration of life, and of the universe, which stem from the Cross . . . from the austerity of the Cross, and from the victory of the Resurrection. There is no contradiction here; these things form an organic whole in the Christian experience. The Eastern Church, while she puts a great emphasis on the 'Life-giving Cross' of the Lord, the Cross on which we all ought to be constantly crucified with Him at the centre of our moral being, also accents the glory of the transfiguration which is already beginning here in this world (although in an incomplete way). This is the significance for us of the lives of saints, the Sacraments of the Church, and of the whole mystery of the Church of God. It is the action of the Holy Spirit, the life of the Holy Spirit in creation.

It is characteristic of the teaching and experience of the Eastern Church on her highest levels that in spite of her very great reticence, her spirit of reserve and sobriety, the breath of the Holy Spirit can be felt within her, the radiance of His glory, and the beginning of the transfiguration of created being. Thus we read passages like the following in the *Lives* of the desert fathers, who were so full of gentleness and the spirit of soberness, balance, and grave discernment.

The abbot Lot came one day to the abbot Joseph and said to him : 'Father, I am fulfilling my rule of life within the measure of my powers. I observe the fasts, I pray, I resort to contemplation,

I keep silence, and try to purify my senses. What must I do now?'
The older man got up and held his hands toward heaven. And
his hands became like ten lighted candles. And he said to the abbot
Lot: 'If you wish to be perfect, then become *all fire*.' [6] The abbot
Vessarion said as he died: 'Like the cherubim and the seraphim,
the monk must become *all eye*.' [7] And in the chapter dedicated to
the great abbot Macarius, here is what we read about two young
anchorites—two brothers whom he had introduced to the solitary
life: 'The younger brother sang five psalms—and at each word
a flame of fire came out of his mouth and went up to heaven. And
in the same way, when the older brother opened his mouth to
sing, a cloud of fire appeared to come out of his mouth and reach
up to heaven.' [8] We find the same burning fire of the Spirit, the
same light, in the life of one of the greatest spiritual men of the
Russian Orthodox Church in the nineteenth century—St. Seraphim
of Sarov. This fire, this light is a figure of transfiguration by the
power of the Holy Spirit, a transfiguration which begins already
in this world, in the realm of exceptional sanctity. Some hints of
this transfigured life are found in the writings of Isaac of Syria
and in some of Macarius's homilies,[9] in Hesychius of Jerusalem,
Philotheus of Sinai and Gregory the Sinaite, but always in the brief-
est allusions, in a spirit of reticence and soberness.[10] Thus St. Isaac
of Syria depicts the beginning of the New Life: 'This will be the
sign that you are nearing the entrance to this country. When grace
begins to open your eyes so that you see things in their essence,
then your eyes will flow with tears which will run down your
cheeks, and the tension of your feelings will be relieved. . . . If
any one teaches you any other thing, do not believe him. . . . Your
heart becomes small like that of a little child, and when you
begin to pray the tears flow. . . .' 'This shows that the luminous
cloud of God is beginning to repose upon the Ark of the Covenant
of your heart. . . .' [11] In the first of Macarius's homilies the holy

---

[6] *Apophtegmata Patrum,* Joseph 6.
[7] ibid., Joseph 7.
[8] *Verba Seniorum,* III, 2, in *Rosweyde, Vitae Patrum,* Antwerp, 1628.
[9] On the problem of the origin of the Macarian writings, see my book
Ostkirche und Mystik, Reinhardt, *Basel-Munich,* 1943, pp. 129–37 and 200–2.
[10] St. Simeon the New Theologian, the great Byzantine mystic of the
eleventh century, describes his spiritual experience in a much more explicit
way, but in this respect he may be regarded as something of an exception.
[11] cf. my book *Ostkirche und Mystik,* p. 143.

soul is compared with the living chariot of Ezekiel's mysterious vision: 'The prophet sees the mystery of the soul ready to receive its Lord and to become the throne of His glory. The soul which the Holy Spirit has chosen for Himself as a throne and lodging place, which He deems worthy to participate in His light, and which He illuminates with the Beauty of His eternal splendour, becomes then all light, all fire, all eye. . . . For the inexpressible beauty of Christ's luminous glory has come upon it and taken up its abode within it.'[12] On these heights 'a man no longer condemns either Jews or Greeks, either sinners or the children of this age.' On the contrary, 'the inner man sees all men through purified eyes, and he rejoices then for the sake of the whole world, and desires with all his heart to love and venerate both Jew and Greek.'[13] Or again, there are these extraordinary words of Isaac on the power of love, the power of compassionate and boundless charity. 'What is a merciful heart? It is the burning of the heart toward all creation—man, fowls and beasts, demons, and whatever exists; so that by the recollection and sight of them the eyes shed tears due to the force of mercy which moves the heart by great compassion. Then the heart becomes weak, and is not able to bear hearing of or beholding injury or any insignificant suffering of any thing in creation. And so therefore even on behalf of irrational beings and the enemies of truth, even for those who do harm to it at all times, he offers prayers with tears that they may be guarded and strengthened—even the various kinds of reptiles —out of the great compassion which is poured out in his heart without measure, after the example of God.'[14] The last word and crown of these sublime states is humble and child-like confidence, the great humility of the heart that feels itself tiny as it stands before God. Nearly at the end of the collection of Isaac's homilies there is a chapter entitled: 'This chapter is full of life.' We read there: 'When thou liest prostrate before God in prayer, then be in thine own eyes as an ant and as the reptiles of the earth and as the beetle. And stammer as one from the country, and speak not before Him with knowledge. Draw near to God and

[12] Macarius, *Homily* 1.
[13] *Homily* 8. 6.
[14] Wensinck, *The Mystical Treatises of Isaac of Nineveh*, trans. from Syrian, Amsterdam, 1923, p. 341.

walk before Him with a child-like mind, that thou mayest be worthy of the paternal care which fathers have for their young children.' [15] Isaac was widely read in Russian monasteries during the Middle Ages.[16]

The creature transfigured! This is the sight of the renewed creature which we see in the faces of the saints; and it is here, incidentally, that we find the hidden significance of the art of the icon. The icon is not a portrait, it seeks rather to evoke the spiritual transfiguration of the creature.[17] Standing at the head of the transfiguration of creation is the Mother of God. The Mother of God occupies a place of high importance in the piety of the Eastern Church. We feel drawn toward her maternal heart, we see in her the first-fruits of creation offered to God, she is our glorified prototype, the one who speaks for us all before the throne of the Son. She is the one who represents mankind in the divine glory, the instrument of our salvation; for she was the most holy and most pure instrument of the Incarnation of the Son of God. Within the piety of the Orthodox Church the Mother of God is never separated from the Son. The unfathomable mystery of the Word of God made flesh is constantly set before the truly Johannine contemplation of the Church, a contemplation full of veneration, of joyous amazement and trembling, when for example the Church addresses her hymns of praise to the Mother of God who is 'more honourable than the cherubim, and beyond compare more glorious than the seraphim.' The angel is sent to the Mother of God to proclaim the Good News, and 'beholding Thy Incarnation, O Lord, he was seized with dread, and spoke to the Virgin in these words: Rejoice, for thou art the source of joy. Rejoice, for thou art the salvation of the fallen Adam. Rejoice, for thou hast dried the tears of Eve. Rejoice, O Sublimity inaccessible to the thought of men. Rejoice, O Depth unfathomable even for the eyes of angels. Rejoice, for thou art the throne of the King of Majesty. Rejoice, for thou bearest Him who bears the universe. Rejoice,

[15] *The Mystical Treatises,* p. 352.
[16] See the remarkable book by the Russian historian B. Ikonikov, *A Study of the Influence of Byzantium on the History of Russia* (in Russian), Kiev, 1869, p. 233.
[17] cf. the small book by the celebrated Russian philosopher Prince Eugene Trubetskoy, *On the Religious Philosophy of the Russian Icon* (German trans., *Die religiose weltanschauung der altrussischen skonenmalerer,* 1929, Paderborn).

O Star that heralds the coming of the Sun. Rejoice, O Womb in which God becomes Man. Rejoice, thou by whom man hast been renewed. . . .'

The veneration of the most Holy Mother of God plays a tremendous role, as we shall see, in the piety of the Russian people, for in her the condescension and mercy of God are manifested.

.　　.　　.

As the field of action of the Holy Spirit, as the beginning of the sanctification of creation, the Church is the context and premise of this whole life of piety. As the great mystical body enlivened by the Holy Spirit the Church is one of the fundamental themes of Russian religious philosophy. The action of the sanctifying Spirit in the life of the Church of God is manifested on many occasions, at every step on the path of spiritual experience, both individual and corporate. It is manifested with a special power in the Sacraments of the Church. Let us say here just a few words about the Sacrament of Holy Communion, the Eucharist.

As with the Roman Catholic Church, the Eucharist is at the very centre of Orthodox religious life, both of individual Christians and of the great community of the faithful. It is as it were a synthesis of the whole of religious experience, the whole 'philosophy' and life of the Church. It is like a great river, a sea, where the different currents, the various aspects of the religious life are joined together and formed into one.

The Lord who is coming to His own; the Presence of the Lord.

These words can in a way serve as a summary of or introduction to the riches of Eucharistic experience. He really comes and is really present in His immaculate Body and precious Blood—the Eastern Church says—in the true Body and true Blood with which He suffered and in which He was raised from the dead, in the glorified and transfigured Body of His Resurrection. This is the mystery which staggers the mind and goes beyond all conception, unfathomable and at the same time completely real, the mystery of the Coming and the Presence of the Resurrected One, of the glorified Lord, Priest and (at the same time) Victim, whose Sacrifice is continually offered to the Heavenly Father. At the same time He comes to His faithful ones, to give Himself to them as nourishment, a true and real nourishment possessing a regenerating and purifying power which vivifies and 'deifies' both soul and body.

In the Orthodox Church the prayers before Communion begin with these words: 'Let Thy holy Body, O merciful Lord, and Thy most precious Blood become for me the bread of eternal life, and also the healing of my many sicknesses.' 'Heal, O Lord,' the prayer continues, 'the wounds of my soul, and sanctify me wholly, make me worthy, who am so unworthy, to receive Thy Divine and Mysterious Communion.'

What we receive in the Communion is the 'spiritual pearl,' the 'burning heat of His Body,' the 'Divine Blood.' This is a 'terrible mystery,' the 'divine mystery,' the 'most pure and dreadful mystery,' the 'immortal and divine mystery.' It is the divine fire: 'I am afraid that in receiving this fire I shall melt like wax and be consumed like grass. O, Terrible Mystery! O, the mercy of God! How can I, who am so corrupted, communicate in the Divine Body and Blood, and thereby become incorruptible?' 'This is the Christ, taste and see. For the Lord, after being offered once in sacrifice to the Father, is continually offered as He sanctifies those who communicate in Him.' 'Let Thy Body and precious Blood become for me as fire and light, O my Saviour, consuming the substance of sin, burning up the thorns of passion, and illuminating my entire being.'

This Communion is completely true and real, physical and at the same time spiritual, embracing my whole being, purifying my soul and planting in my body the seed of life eternal, of the resurrection to come. But there is nothing 'magical' or 'mechanical' in this Communion. It is imbued with an ethical quality, it is founded on moral presuppositions: it is the soul of a sinner that cries out from its abyss to the mercy of the Lord. A moral tension, an anguished search for purity, and a profound contrition, penetrate all the Liturgy and prayers before Communion. For the soul is conscious of its fundamental unworthiness, its weakness and frailty. It is only with these feelings of utmost humility, with the cry of a repentant sinner who sees himself as he really is and condemns himself, it is only with such feelings that we can approach the Lord's Table. 'I know, O my Lord,' says St. Basil in his prayer before Communion, 'that I am receiving Thy immaculate Body and Thy precious Blood unworthily, that I am guilty, that I eat and drink to my condemnation, not discerning Thy Body and Blood . . . yet in spite of this I approach Thy table, committing myself to Thy great goodness.' 'I believe, my Lord, and I confess,' says Chrysostom, 'that Thou art truly the Christ who has come into the world to save sinners, of whom I am the first.' 'My Lord and my God, I know that I am not worthy, and I am ashamed that Thou shouldst desire to come under the roof of the temple of my soul, for it has fallen into ruin and desolation, and there is no place there where Thou canst rest thy head. But as Thou hast humbled Thyself in descending from the heights of heaven for the sake of man's salvation, so deign now to humble Thyself to the depths of my unworthiness' (Chrysostom).

The Lord comes not only to the individual soul, but also to His whole Church, and the mystical encounter in the Sacrament of the Eucharist is not only individual, but individual and corporate. What takes place here occurs above all within the individual's inner religious experience, but at the same time there is here a reality which involves the whole fullness of existence, the soul, and the body, eternity, and the course of history, all mankind, and the whole of creation. For this is a mystical experience of a quite exceptional order, corresponding to the very essence of the Good News. It is indissolubly connected with *historical* reality, with the *humanity* of our Lord, i.e. with a completely tangible and concrete reality, with the true humanity of the One who suffered and was crucified, and was raised again and transfigured in glory. The whole structure of the Liturgy is simply an expectation of the glorified Lord, is simply the preparation and the consummation of His coming to the faithful. He comes to His Church as the King of Majesty, shining in glory, He who suffered, and is alive, who is raised from the dead and surrounded by angelic powers. . . . For 'Lo, the King of glory enters,' the Eastern Church sings in her Liturgy of the Presanctified Gifts, 'Lo, the mysterious sacrifice is accomplished, and solemnly brought in. Let us approach with faith and love, that we may participate in life eternal. Alleluia.' And these same themes recur in the hymn of the 'cherubim' in the usual Liturgy (of St. John Chrysostom): '. . . let us lay aside

44

all earthly cares, that we may receive the King of all, invisibly accompanied by angelic hosts.' He is Sovereign, King and Lord. 'Blessed be the Kingdom of the Father, and of the Son, and of the Holy Spirit,' are the words with which this Liturgy begins.

We have in this boundless glory of the Risen One, the King of Glory, a commemoration of His passion and sacrifice. It may be said that the two fundamental and essential elements in the experience of the Christian Church are joined together in the Eucharist. The Lord's death is constantly recalled in the memory of the Church, constantly 'represented,' in the literal sense of the word, i.e. made present. This is the foundation, the corner stone, on which the whole edifice is built. Without this historical reality, without this sacrifice, this death and victory over death, there is no salvation. This is the 'evangelical' moment of the Eucharist, the living and uninterrupted tradition of the apostolic message, the *depositum fidei*. But in addition, this sacrifice is *made present* for the faithful, not as a simple commemoration but as a real presence. Not in the sense that the sacrifice of Golgotha is infinitely repeated by the Church. There is no need for repetition, the death of the Lord which took place 'once' on Golgotha was completely sufficient for our salvation. But this voluntary sacrifice which took place 'once for all' is perpetually offered to the Father in eternity by the Lamb of God, as the Seer tells us in the fifth chapter of Revelation: 'And I looked, and behold, between the throne and the four living creatures I saw the Lamb standing, as it were slain' (Rev. 5: 6: ἀρνίον ἑστηκὸς ὡς ἐσφαγμένον). It is not that He comes down from heaven to be sacrificed by a priest, but rather that we, i.e. the Church, are lifted up in the Sacrament of Communion to the level of the heavenly altar on which the Lamb of God is offering, from all eternity, that saving death which was consummated on Golgotha. This is why the element of divine *glory,* of the celestial altar with the angelic hosts covering their faces with their wings in dread before the inexpressible mystery of the divine sacrifice, is so emphasized by the Eastern Church. We need only mention, for example, the homilies of St. John Chrysostom, or his treatise on the priesthood, to be aware of this. We have already indicated the other basic element in the overall experience of the Church, as manifested in the Sacrament of the Eucharist: the constant presence of the Lord in the midst of us. The promise which He gave to the faithful: 'And I shall be with you always, until the end of time'—a promise not limited, needless to say, to the Eucharist—finds here its most tangible, concrete and wonderful expression. It is the eternally 'catholic' element in the Church which is revealed here with special force.

Thus the interior experience, the interior encounter of the soul with its Lord as King, Healer, merciful Saviour—and that 'Christian realism,' historical and at the same time mystical, that is based on a concrete fact belonging to history; and the proclamation of the Lord's death, the 'representation' of His life-giving death as the source of our salvation and of His constant presence in the midst of us—the presence of the Risen and Glorified One, the Victim, Priest and King of Glory; and further the individual element, and the corporate experience of the Church—all this is united in the Sacrament of the Eucharist. To return to the corporate motif— the experience of the *great communion of the faithful* (both the living and the dead) united around the Eucharistic altar is encountered with special force in this Sacrament of Holy Communion. St. Paul's words have their confirmation here: 'We are all one body, for we have communion in one bread.'

I will not make use of material which can be found in a great number of texts of the Orthodox Liturgies to illustrate further this experience of the great communion of the faithful. I wish only to emphasize once again the *cosmic* moment of the Eucharist. The Eucharist is the first-fruit of the sanctification of all creation, as St. Irenaeus said, this bread taken from the fields and this wine taken from the vineyards, becoming the true Body and Blood of the Lord. We could dwell at length on this cosmic moment of the Eucharist, could cite texts, for example, from St. Irenaeus, St. Ephraim of Syria, from the Liturgies of Jerusalem and Alexandria. It is enough here to remind ourselves again of the great importance of this aspect, i.e., the transfiguration and sanctification of all creation, already begun, already given in principle, potentially, in the facts of the Incarnation, death and Resurrection of the Son of God. As we have seen, these cosmic overtones, as revealed to the eyes of faith are extremely characteristic of the piety of the Orthodox Church.

And finally there is the *eschatological* moment—the echo of St. Paul's words: 'You commemorate the Lord's death until He comes.' This too is a living element in the piety of the Church. In a prayer (taken from the Paschal Office) which the priests say before the altar after having received Communion, we read: 'O Father, O sublime and most holy Christ! O Wisdom, the Word and power of God! Grant that we may participate in Thee in a way yet more perfect in the inextinguishable light of Thy Kingdom to come.'

In order to know the Orthodox Church in her depths—despite all the imperfections and weaknesses of the empirical reality—it is necessary to know the spiritual struggle of the saints, their great humility, and the Church's Eucharistic experience, as the first-fruits of a new order of things not only coming in the future, but also already coming here in this world in a hidden way; to see them as the fruit of the life-giving Cross and Resurrection.

CHAPTER THREE

THE ROLE OF RITE AND RELIGIOUS CUSTOM IN THE LIFE OF THE RUSSIAN PEOPLE; ABERRATIONS IN THE RELIGIOUS LIFE

LET us return to the Russian people. They found an equilibrium or axis in the life of the Church. That chaotic element, the exuberance of feelings and sometimes even revolt against all established order, against all law and regulation (represented in the mind of the people by the figures of the great popular brigands, such as Stenka Razin or any one of the ferocious bandits of the Volga region and the Brynsk forests), that chaotic element was counterbalanced by the settled pattern of religious usage and custom, by the framework of the Church's ritual, by family traditions sanctified by the religious life. There was here a quite different ideal, opposed to the lack of order and moral equilibrium and the ideal of brazen audacity; here was an ideal developed out of a spiritual discipline influencing both the soul and also outward behaviour. This ideal found its expression in such words as *blagolepie, istovost, blago-obrazie,* words that are difficult to translate but which signify a penetration of the entire being by a spiritual order imparting a *religious beauty* to the whole of one's conduct and manner of life, a quality that is humble and at the same time full of a sense of religious responsibility and interior dignity. Here is an example taken at random from Russian literature, the scene from one of the fragments of Leo Tolstoy's unfinished novel *The Decembrists,* in which the old peasant Tikhonovna is going on foot to Moscow (at the beginning of the nineteenth century) to submit a petition on behalf of her husband, who has been unjustly imprisoned. Having rested at the home of acquaintances, she sets out for the great mansion of her owners, who live in Moscow, the wealthy and aristocratic Chernyshev family, a house surrounded by outbuildings, courtyards and gardens. She enters the kitchen of the vast servants' quarters, and feels lost and intimidated. For her this was a venture into 'another world.' The younger servants look at her mockingly. But she does not lose her presence of mind. Humble, modest and full of natural dignity, in her peasant garb, with white bands wrapped round her legs, she first bows deeply three times before the holy icons in the corner, and only then bows respectfully to all those present. And suddenly all the scoffing stops. This was the same ancient custom mentioned by foreign travellers coming to Russia prior to the time of Peter the Great—for example, Baron von Herberstein, who visited the court of Moscow in 1517 and 1526, and Baron von Meyerbeer, who stayed there from 1660 to 1665. Immediately upon entering someone's house, even the house of very highly placed persons, one bowed deeply first before the icons, which represented the presence of the invisible God. The honours given to men came after; one began by giving honour to God.

Let us dwell for a moment on the religious traditions of the family. At the heart of this tradition there is the *parental blessing,* something which is found all over the world in families with a Christian background. The old Russian epic ballads or *byliny,* corresponding to the French *chansons de geste,* often depict heroes asking for the blessing of their parents. . . .

This is not a verdant oak bowing to the ground,
These are not little papery leaves being scattered round,
This is the son bowed down before his father,
Begging for his benediction.

. . . these are the words of the epic ballad about the exploits of the great legendary Russian hero: Ilya Muromets. Then there is the hot-headed and adventurous Basil Buslayev, with his wild, bandit's heart, often without faith or sense of law, the typical representative in Russian medieval ballads of the impetuous and enterprising young man from the great and powerful republic of Novgorod. Even Buslayev bows respectfully before his mother, it is she alone whom he venerates and still obeys, and to whom he turns for counsel and a blessing.

49

D

Vasinka (diminutive of Basil) decides he'll go to Jerusalem.
Vasinka goes to ask a blessing of his mother.
He bows his fiery head down to the damp ground.
This is not a white birch bowing down,
These are not little silken leaves that scatter on the ground.
This is Vasinka bowed down before his mother.

The concrete symbol of this paternal benediction and of the continuity of this family religious tradition down through the generations is the ancestral icon, this holy image, about which we have already spoken. Just as the family Bible was passed on from one generation to another in old Protestant (Huguenot) families, and was the sign of the spiritual unity of the family down through the centuries, so too the icon inherited from one's ancestors often represented the spiritual link between the various generations of a Russian family. When a young couple set up a new household, they would bring into their new home the 'paternal blessing,' i.e. the ancestral icon with which their parents had blessed them, and with which the grandfather or great-grandfather had previously been blessed by his own parents at the time of his own marriage. These ancestral icons were often preserved with awe in old families which had maintained their position and identity, in those families among the nobility which were imbued with religious tradition, in the great old merchant families, in lesser middle class families too, and in many peasant families, especially in families of 'Old Believers,' who observed the ancient traditions of a religious culture with jealous and sometimes fanatical devotion.

Thus the ancient icon with which Prince Ivan Dolgoruky (a great favourite of the young emperor Peter II, who was executed about 1730 at the command of the Empress Anna) had blessed his son was kept in one branch of the Dolgoruky family right down to the time of the Soviet Revolution. The icon of the *tsarskaya nevesta*—i.e. Marie Khlopov, who at the beginning of the seventeenth century was officially betrothed to Tsar Michael Romanov, but was removed from the court as a result of palace intrigue before the marriage was celebrated—has been kept in the Ermolov family; this icon represented the 'blessing' of the parents of the bride to be. In one branch of the family of Prince Golitsin and later in the Arseniev family an ancient and much honoured icon has been reverently preserved, dating from the seventeenth century; the famous Prince Alexander Menshikov, exiled to Siberia in the eighteenth century under Peter II, used this icon to bless his daughter on her marriage, during the time that he was in exile.

In the important work of R. Tereshchenko, *The Customs of the Russian People*, which appeared a little over a century ago, we have a description of the family rites for the blessing of young married couples by parents in peasant homes, as it was done in various provinces. In the district of Nizhni Novgorod, for example, the rite was carried out in the following manner. Before the departure of the bride and groom to the church, each of them received their parents' blessing in the paternal house. A table was placed beneath the icons in the holy corner and was covered with a white cloth, then some salt, some rye bread and some white bread were placed on the table, candles and an oil lamp were lighted before the icons, and all would pray there with the bridegroom. Then the betrothed would be led before his parents, standing by the table, the father holding the icon, the mother holding the rye bread. Three times the betrothed would bow before the parents, asking for their blessing, and then the father and mother would bless him in turn, first with the icon and then with the bread, kissing the betrothed three times. I am presenting here only the general outline of this rite, which was sometimes quite elaborate.

The blessing was also given before a departure on a journey or a long separation, when, for example, a son or husband left for war. There were many family traditions in all social classes concerning the power of blessings and a mother's prayer to protect her child in perils and temptations. Sometimes a small icon or medal hung by the mother around the neck of her son would, during battle, deflect a bullet and save a young man's life. Tolstoy's great-grandfather, Prince Sergius Volkonsky, was miraculously saved in this way during the Seven Years' War. A beautiful scene in Tolstoy's *War and Peace* was inspired by this family tradition. Prince Andrew is taking leave of his sister before leaving for the front. He is an unbeliever. But she begs him to let her hang around his neck a small image of Christ which their grandfather had worn during battle. ' "Even against your will, He will save you and have pity on you, and will convert you, for truth and peace come from Him only," she said in a voice trembling with emotion. She held up before her brother, with a solemn gesture, an ancient oval image of the Lord, a tarnished tin image set in gold, on a thin golden chain. She made the sign of the Cross, kissed the image and held it out to Andrew. "Please, do it for me. . . ." Her large eyes shone with goodness and a hidden light. Her brother was about to take the image, but she stopped him. He understood what she expected of him, and also made the sign of the Cross, and kissed the image.'

General D. S. Dokhturov, a hero of the War of 1812, wrote to his wife just after the battle of Borodino (where he had taken command of the left flank of the Russian army after Prince Bagration was mortally wounded), 'I thank you, my darling, for sending me the holy image. I am going to wear it against my chest. I see clearly God's great mercy toward me. In terrible danger He has saved me. I thank the Most High.'

Family custom, the rituals of daily life and also of life's more solemn moments were all influenced and marked by the prayers and rites of the Church. There were many of these traditions in old Russia, even among the cultivated classes (I am thinking here of the *truly* cultivated, i.e. those who had combined their spiritual and religious tradition with the culture of modern Europe). And what an interior warmth, what a feeling of peace and security, what a hidden and profound meaning and spiritual purpose this gave to everyday life! The family became a vital focus of the religious life.

When a member of the family left on a trip, the whole family —including the servants—would gather together in silence. They would remain silent for several minutes. Then the eldest person— the father, or the mother, or the eldest brother—would rise and make the sign of the Cross, and every one would make the sign of the Cross upon themselves while facing the icon, with a silent prayer. Then a mutual blessing was exchanged. In families which have kept their traditions down to the present day, the children, when they come each evening to say good night to their parents, still receive their special blessing. In each case it is the life of the Church, her liturgical and sacramental life, which has penetrated and profoundly influenced the life of the family. There is too the first confession—children usually make it at the age of seven in the Orthodox Church. In pious families it is the mother who prepares the child, who explains to him the meaning of the Sacrament of Repentance, the necessity of making an effort to better one's life and serve the Lord, it is she who prepares him to receive the Holy Communion worthily, with humility and trembling, with a contrite heart. And then there are the purifying days of Lent, especially the first and last weeks, and Holy Week, when the mother goes to church with her children, when the whole schedule of the day is adapted to the services of the Church, when the last stages of our Lord's earthly life before His Passion are relived step by step; and then comes the Passion, His death on the Cross, His burial, and His glorious Resurrection. The life of pious families used to be full of echoes of this cultic life, one was carried along on the great stream of the Church's life. The fasts were observed—no butter, no milk, no meat, no eggs. The night of Good Friday to Holy Saturday was spent at the service of the 'Burial of Christ,' when the whole church glowed with innumerable lighted candles held by the faithful, when the people took part in the solemn procession around the church, when the linen cloth or 'shroud' (*plashchanitsa*) depicting the Lord lying in the tomb was carried on the head of the priest above the thronging crowd. And the night of Easter, which was the greatest, most joyous and most intimate family festival that Christian Russia has ever known! After the all-night service, after this outburst of triumphant joy, when the bells in their towers rang out across the Russian land from midnight on, when the bonfires, the illumination of the churches, the lighted candles, the alternating chants of the choirs, and the greetings with the Kiss of Peace all translated the gladness of Christ's victory over death, people would gather again at home around the sumptuous Easter table (decorated and well provided on this night even in the most humble homes). This was not just a treat after the long days of Lent, but also a feast of joy and spiritual communion between the members of the family and household, a pure and innocent human joy, illumined by the rays of the Lord's victory. The life of the family—on these warm and lively occasions—was brightened and made glad, on the background of the Easter glory. A little 'gleam' or ray of the transfiguration would come for a few minutes into the ordinary life of man. This Easter night lived through in the bosom of the family is one of the greatest treasures of the religious and family tradition of Russia.

. . .

This ideal of the family has been badly shaken by the compulsory secularization of life in Soviet Russia, but in fact it was threatened long before the Soviet Revolution. We can see its elaboration and formulation, an often rigid, narrow and one-sided formulation, in the medieval period. Before the Reform of Peter the Great the whole life and culture of Russia, including family life, had evolved on a sacral background, on the background of the life of the Church—but often only in theory.

We know that all too often human life corresponds only slightly to its own ideal, and medieval Russia was no exception. It was full of imperfections and sins and very often quite 'pagan' in its mores (one thinks of the endless carousals, the manifestations of brutality —despite the basic good nature of the Russian people—and of the strange and sometimes savage superstitions). But it should be emphasized that this life was often *sacral and Christian* in its inspiration and implicit assumptions, and the ideal did not fail to influence reality, if only in a very imperfect way. The religious view of life was not always free, as we have said, from narrowness and rigidity. Its most characteristic formulation in medieval Russia is found in the celebrated *Domostroi,* which dates from the fifteenth–sixteenth century, and in its most famous redaction written by the Archpriest Sylvester, the godly and judicious counsellor of Ivan the Terrible during the glorious and still virtuous period of his life.

This treatise is in part compiled from ancient sources—passages drawn from the Wisdom literature of the Old Testament, the works of the holy Fathers, especially St. John Chrysostom, from the *Lives* of the Saints, and also from certain earlier Russian works, such as the *Testament* of Prince Vladimir Monomakh addressed to his children (dating from the first quarter of the twelfth century). Some parts seem to have their origins in the great republic of

Novgorod, and probably depict the economic life of a great boyar household in Novgorod at the end of the fifteenth century; and finally, other sections reflect the situation in Moscow at the middle of the sixteenth century. The whole work, however, has an internal unity. The spirit animating the *Domostroi* is not, as it has been the custom to say in Russian literary circles in the last hundred years, a sullen and misanthropic spirit, full of an intolerant and gloomy fanaticism. This judgment is based mainly on two passages. One deals with the question of the education of children: 'Do not be lax in beating your child; if you beat him with a stick he will not die, but will be better withal, for you lay stripes on his body but deliver his soul from death. . . .' 'Do not give a free reign to his wishes in youth, but as long as he is still growing lay blows on his body, otherwise he will become hardened in a headstrong way of life and will not obey you' (Chapter 17). And again, in Chapter 38, household discipline is inculcated with the most detailed instructions: how everything ought to be held in great esteem, how the tables, the dishware, the platters, the pots, the ladles, etc., ought to be washed in hot water three times each in the morning, after dinner and in the evening; that in the same way the buckets, basins, pails, caldrons, pitchers, tubs, strainers, etc., ought to be not only washed but also scraped and rubbed until they are perfectly in order, and that also the benches, windows, doors, floors and all furniture should be kept impeccably clean, frequently washed, rubbed, dusted, scraped, swept, etc. After all these recommendations the author goes on to the interior discipline of the servants, children, and one's spouse. If something is not done well, if the wife does not manage to keep discipline among the servants, the husband must explain to his wife how it ought to be done, and instruct her in this task. If she tries to follow his instructions he ought to show her his approval and affection. If on the contrary the wife does not take care and does not follow her husband's precepts, then he must draw her aside and reprimand her; after which he should again show affection toward her (*pozhalovati*). All this must be done 'with love.' 'But if the wife or son or daughter does not listen to the reprimands, and has no fear, and does not do what the husband, father or mother teaches them to do—then punishment must be applied with a "lash"

55

(*pletka*) according to the fault committed. This must be done not in the presence of other persons, but alone; and after the punishment the husband must speak some edifying words to his wife and show her his affection; and there should be no provoking to anger, neither by the wife of the husband, nor by the husband of the wife.' There follows a description of the method of beating, which must never be done in the eyes, or on the face, or in the region of the chest, nor with a stick, or anything made of iron or wood, nor must the husband ever strike in a moment of anger, for much evil can follow. The beating should be administered only with the 'plet' (a kind of lash made of fabric or thongs), 'and only in the case of a great fault; and the beating should be done politely(!) with a small lash, while holding the wife by the hands, and after the punishment some instruction should be given, and then the husband should add: "There is no place now for offence. Let no one take offence at anything that has been done...." ' (Chapter 38).

This is undoubtedly a very 'medieval' and authoritarian way of teaching, and it cannot fail to strike us as rather barbarous. But the treatise as a whole is not of this character. It is imbued in fact with a feeling of the fear of God, of moral responsibility toward God and neighbour, with a sense of moral discipline which must be expressed in the whole external structure of life, and above all it is inspired by a call for active charity toward all afflicted or distressed people. Thus we read, in Chapter 6: 'Visit those who are in the monasteries, the hospitals and those who are confined in prison, and bring alms to them according to your means, and anything else they may need. And when you see their misery and pain, help them as much as you can. And do not despise, do not neglect the one who is suffering, the poor, the needy, and the beggar; bring him into your home, give him something to eat, and drink, and something to wear, in all love, and with a pure conscience.' In the appendix to the *Domostroi*—the epistle of the priest Sylvester to his son—we find similar admonitions. In support of his counsel Sylvester draws his son's attention to his own example: 'I have never willingly neglected caring for beggars and those without shelter, the poor, and the afflicted. Those in prison, military captives and debtors, I have released on payment;

the hungry I have fed. All my serfs I have freed, and provided them with the means to live. I have also bought the freedom of serfs belonging to others. All our old serfs are now free and living in their own homes in prosperity, praying to God for us. . . . Now all our servants are free people who live with us of their own accord. You have seen how many orphans, serfs and poor people, men and women, in Novgorod and in Moscow, I have fed and raised to the age of maturity, giving them instruction according to their abilities; many of them I have had taught how to read, write and sing; others how to paint holy images; still others in the work of copying books, and others in the silversmith trade, or some other, and others I have set up in business. Your mother too has taught and instructed many girls, orphans and poor children, and, providing them with a dowry, has found husbands for them. For young men too we have found brides from good homes. Many of our young men now have the rank of priest or deacon, or are readers or teachers in the Church. . . .'

Another feature which catches the reader's attention is the emphasis placed on gentleness, patience, goodwill and humility in one's relations with others. The bearing of injuries and injustices in all humility, not repaying evil for evil, but making an effort to be reconciled with men by gentleness and good deeds done to them. And then there are all kinds of counsels of a primarily practical nature—how to buy, prepare and preserve all sorts of provisions, directions for the kitchen, the wine cellar, etc. All this does not concern us here. These books of instructions, dealing with household management and containing precepts as much moral as practical, were in fact widespread also in the West during the Middle Ages and the Renaissance. A whole series of works of this type are found in Italy (the Hermit of Bari in the thirteenth century, E. Colonna; Agnolo Pandolfini in the fifteenth century); in Germany (Vridank's 'Bescheidenheit'); in France ('Le Menagier de Paris' of the fifteenth century); and in Bohemia. What is important for us here is to note how the Church's influence penetrated all the usages and customs of family life.

After its general religious and moral admonitions, the *Domostroi* gives a very detailed description of the way the cult of the Church ought to enter into the life of the household. 'In his house every Christian must place holy and sacred images on the walls of every room, in all reverence, with ornaments and holders in which candles can be lighted before the holy images whenever God is praised. After the service the candles are put out, the icons are recovered with a veil in order to protect them from dust. . . . They are to be cleaned with a duster or a damp sponge. And such rooms must be kept in all decency . . .' (Chapter 8). In another chapter we find a schedule of daily prayers (Vespers, Compline, the night prayers and Matins) which the father must read and chant with the members of his family and all the inhabitants of the household, including the servants, in the family chapel. 'And at midnight it is necessary to rise secretly and beg God with tears to pardon our sins . . .' (Chapter 12). The whole course of life must be set in this framework of prayer, prayer is constantly impressed. Every manual task, every undertaking must begin with an invocation of God: 'After washing your hands carefully, you should bow three times before the holy images,' and then say a short prayer and make the sign of the Cross (Chapter 10).

One may well ask if this was only an ideal, or if it is an authentic description of real life. From the evidence we have, it was an ideal. As such, however, it could not fail to have some influence on life. The *Domostroi* often tells us that this is the way things are done 'among pious people,' 'among good and sensible people,' etc. The compiler therefore has certain examples before his eyes.[1] And we know, from many ancient sources as well as from more recent evidence, how much a pious ritualism (especially among the Old Believers) could influence the course of Russian life, both individual and corporate, and to what extent there existed in Russia—alongside moral laxity and a frequent lack of discipline—an area of life that was regulated and inspired by an inner discipline, illuminated by liturgical beauty, and strengthened by the influence of *the rites of the Church.*

I would like to present here just a few examples drawn from the life of ancient Russia. The Frenchman Margeret, Instructor of the Russian army at the beginning of the seventeenth century (1600–6), wrote an extremely interesting book on his return to France, on the request of King Henry IV, in which he appears as

[1] On this subject see Prof. Porfiriev's *History of Russian Literature.*

an intelligent and reliable observer. He describes the way in which the rather touching custom of 'Forgiveness' was observed in old Moscow on the eve of Lent (it was apparently practised then throughout the whole week preceding Lent). This custom has been preserved down to the twentieth century, but is disappearing and is limited now to the 'Sunday of Forgiveness' and observed only by those who remain faithful to this cultic tradition.[2] In those days it was practised among all classes of people, and conducted in public with great solemnity. 'They go about visiting one another, kissing one another, offering good wishes, and asking forgiveness if they have offended one another in word or deed; even when meeting on the streets and without having ever seen one another before (meaning that they asked forgiveness of perfect strangers), kissing one another and saying: *"Prosti mene, pozhalui"*—'Forgive me, please." To which the reply was made: *"Bozh tebe prosti,"* which meant "God forgive you, and forgive me too." '[3] Other travellers also testify to the religious fervour of the Russian people. When a Russian who was travelling found an open church on his road, he would enter and remain there until the end of the service. If the church was closed, he would often kneel down before the door and pray, with his head bowed. Olearius (who visited Russia in 1633, 1636 and 1638–9) tells us that at the sight of a church or even simply of a Cross Russians never failed to make the sign of the Cross and say a short prayer: 'Have mercy upon me, O Lord.' [4]

Here, finally, is a characteristic incident from the life of the pious Tsar Alexis Mikhailovich. Returning in the dead of winter from

---

[2] For a description of this custom among the common people and petty bourgeoisie of Moscow toward the end of the nineteenth century—in the '80s—see the remarkable book of the Russian writer Ivan Shmelyov, *The Year of the Lord.*

[3] *Etat de l'Empire de Russie et du grand Duché de Moscovie,* Capt. Margeret, Paris, 1669, p. 35.

[4] L. P. Rushchinsky, *The Religious Life of Russians* as reflected in the works of foreign authors of the sixteenth and seventeenth centuries, Moscow, 1871, pp. 91–2 (in Russian); Adam Olearius, *Ausfuhrliche Beschreibung der Kunbaren Reyss nach Moscow und Persien,* 1646, (I quote from the Russian translation of P. Barson, Moscow, 1870, p. 27); Th. Warmund, *La Religion ancienne et moderne des Muscovites,* Cologne, 1698, p. 59. Campense, 1525 (Russian trans. in *Library of Foreign Authors Writing on Russia,* P. Kolistratov, 1847, Vol. I); Ulfeld, *Legatio Moscovitica,* Frankfort, 1627 (cf. A. Starczewski, *Historiae Ruthenicae Scriptores exteri saeculi* XVI, Berlin, 1842, Vol. I); Tanner, *Legatio Polono-Lituanica in Moscoviam,* 1680, p. 69.

his victorious campaign against Poland, he visited the Novo-
Devichi monastery as he was approaching Moscow. The icons are
brought forward as he comes near, he reverences them with three
deep bows, almost touching the snow with his forehead. All the
clergy from all the churches of the capital, with their church
banners and crosses, and at their head the two Patriarchs (the
Patriarch of Moscow and the Patriarch of Antioch, who was a
guest of the Tsar) had formed in a solemn procession, and were
waiting for the Tsar near the city's 'Earthen Rampart.' While still
at a distance, the Tsar left his carriage and advanced on foot to
meet the procession.[5] Still more moving was the pious humility
with which Tsar Alexis came, in 1652, to meet the relics of the
holy Metropolitan Philip of Moscow (murdered under Ivan the
Terrible) when they were being solemnly transferred to that city.
The Tsar wanted to make an act of public repentance—in the
name of the Russian monarchy—for the death of the great saint,
who had defended the truth and fallen victim to Ivan's sacrilegious
cruelty. This solemn entry into Moscow of the relics of the murdered
Metropolitan was bound to produce a deep impression on the soul
of the people.[6] The influence of the ritual and prayer of the Church
on public and political life, especially at moments of national
disaster or joy following deliverance from peril, has been constant
all through Russian history, down to the most recent times. It is
enough to recall the *molebni* (Te Deum's) sung before the sacred
images of the Virgin which were carried in procession around the
walls of besieged cities, or sung on the field of battle at decisive
moments in Russian history (for example, on the eve of the battle
of Borodino).

For the people as a whole, as well as for the individual and
the family, the ritual of the Church could bring a message full of
meaning, pointing to an invisible, all-powerful and merciful
Presence, who condescends to come to us, to deliver us, to raise
us up morally and fill all corners of our life with a sanctifying
breath. Let us add that there was also the danger that the ritual
could be 'petrified' and 'absolutized,' i.e. it could be regarded as a

[5] See *The Travels of Macarius Patriarch of Antioch,* written by his attending
Archdeacon Paul of Aleppo in Arabia, trans. by F. C. Balfour, London, 1829–36.
[6] See the letter of Tsar Alexis to Prince Odoevsky, March 9th, 1652, published in *Akty arkeegraficheskye,* Vol. IV, p. 491.

holy reality in itself, containing absolute value within itself, a value lying precisely in *this* verbal formulation, in *this* sacred gesture, these latter being regarded as things immutable and incorruptible. This view, to which the Russian people were brought by certain ritualistic traditions imported from Byzantium, was a view which often found fertile soil in the lack of religious instruction among the common people, and it was to play a fatal role in the religious troubles of the seventeenth century.

We ought not to close our eyes to the dangers which have come as a result of according an often exaggerated significance to rite; to the dangers of *extreme ritualism*. This danger hangs over the whole religious history of Russia and it has often been the source of aberrations in Russian piety. When accidental forms of cult are identified with divine reality religion becomes coloured by super-stition. Although the icon was a symbol of the divine Presence and of the Church's blessing in the bosom of the family and in daily life, and an object of veneration founded on the dogmatic teaching of Orthodoxy, it sometimes gave birth in medieval Russia to strange and superstitious practices. Travellers in Russia during the seventeenth century have reported that each parishioner had his own icon in the church, which he had brought from home and placed on a shelf. During the service each one turned toward his own icon and prayed before it, often without paying attention to the liturgy of the Church. He allowed no one else to pray before his icon for fear that 'with his prayers' the other person might 'catch for himself, like a thief, all the graces of God flowing out of it, to which he alone was entitled, as the owner of the icon.' When, during the Liturgy, the Holy Gifts were displayed to the faithful in solemn procession, each parishioner would turn his eyes toward the altar. Then after the doors of the iconostas were closed they would turn again to their icons. The Tsar himself worshipped in this same way. All this is based on the accounts of Baron von Meyerbeer (a Roman Catholic, and ambassador of the German Emperor at the court of Alexis Mikhailovich from 1661–5),[7] the German Lutheran Theophilus Wermund,[8] and the Englishman Perry, who lived in Russia under Peter the Great

[7] *Iter in Moscoviam*, pp. 28, 51, 1094.
[8] *Universa religio Moscovitarum*, p. 85.

(1698–1711).[9] The Russians had a predilection for liturgical pomp. They were carried away by beautiful hymns, beautiful voices—especially the fine voices of the deacons. Those wonderful deacons' voices! The middle class merchants especially, still rooted —throughout the nineteenth century—in the old cultic tradition, and above all the great old merchant families, had a passion for fine (sometimes almost superhuman) bass voices which, like peels of thunder or the rumble of huge casks, would make the window panes rattle, and brought a feeling of delight and awe to the hearts of the faithful. This predilection for deacons with tremendous voices is described with great charm and humour in a masterpiece by Nicolas Leskov, 'Pillage' (*Grabyezh*), a story which turns on an artistic duel between two deacons who are the candidates for the deacon's office in a parish looking for an extraordinary bass voice.

Too much attention was often given to richness of decoration. For example, the habit of covering over icons with gold decorative vestments—often studded with precious stones—which concealed the picture as a whole and left only the faces and hands of the figures in view, was a custom which began to spread rapidly in the seventeenth century and soon became almost universal, and there can be no doubt that this marked a decline in the great art of Russian iconography, a mechanical externalization of the concept of sacred art. The Russian genius was often carried to extremes, it loved to draw attention to itself, to inspire amazement. This can be seen in the history of church bells. Bells played a tremendous role in the Russian religious life of the sixteenth–seventeenth centuries—so we are told by foreigners who visited Russia during that time. On feast days, we are told, Russians expressed their spiritual gladness by a ringing of bells so overwhelming that it was impossible to converse in the streets. The Archdeacon Paul of Aleppo, who came to Russia in 1653 in the company of the Patriarch Macarius of Antioch, estimated that there were about 40,000 bells in and around Moscow (about 4,000 churches, with approximately ten bells per church). The tower of 'Ivan the Great' alone had fifty bells, twenty-two of them of

[9] *The State of Russia under the Present Czar*, London, 1716. Rushchinsky, op. cit., pp. 44–5.

unusually large size. Russians had a predilection not only for many bells, but also for bells of huge dimension. Some of the bells in Russia were apparently the largest in the world.[10] The largest of all was the gigantic 'Tsar of Bells' which fell to the ground during the reign of Empress Anna, and is still to-day one of the main sights in the Moscow Kremlin.

We shall have occasion to speak again of the profound meaning of liturgical beauty for the religious soul. But we also know how disastrous can be the unbounded and poorly understood attachment to external forms of rite. The great Russian Schism (*raskol*) of the seventeenth century is the sad proof of this fact. The blame for the Schism is very far from being all on the side of the Old Believers. On the contrary, it must be admitted that the blunder committed by the leaders of the Church (the Patriarch Nikon, his colleagues and successors) was even more serious. On both sides an undue significance was attached to often insignificant details of rite, and the dispute was carried on in a malicious party spirit. What increases the responsibility of the Church's leadership for the Schism is that their intolerance was the intolerance of *persecutors*, while the often barbarous and ignorant intolerance of the Old Believers was that of *the persecuted*. If Nikon had tried to accomplish his liturgical reform—which was often ill-founded even from a purely historical viewpoint—in a conciliatory way, the Schism would perhaps never have occurred. The basic cause of the Schism is precisely that both parties regarded ritual details as the immutable verities of dogmatic tradition, although in fact they change during the course of history without really touching the faith. The Patriarch Nikon wanted to introduce—by brute force and with fire and sword—the contemporary Greek rite (in many instances more modern than the rite then preserved in Russia), while the Old Believers saw his action as the work of Anti-Christ (thanks to the ferocious cruelty of his methods), regarded the 'new rite' as a terrible deceit of the devil and the Church's representatives as the devils minions, and were prepared, sometimes with amazing heroism (but a narrow heroism, burning with passionate and savage hatred), to die for the ritual details which they regarded as an integral part of the faith of the fathers. We

[10] Rushchinsky, pp. 67–71.

must always add at once that this quarrel did not remain purely one of ritual, even though the excessive importance attached to rite was its main cause. In each modification of the liturgical texts decreed by Nikon, in each statement of the new ecclesiastical books, the Old Believers began to suspect a hidden meaning, a dogmatic significance which seemed to them heretical and impious. The Petition (*chelobitnaya*) presented in 1665 to Tsar Alexis by the priest Bobrynin, one of the more vigorous and intransigent of the leaders of the sectarians (hence his sobriquet: *Pustosvyat*— 'The False Saint'), is an eloquent example of this reaction.[11] On the other hand the great idea which possessed Nikon and the Tsar Alexis was the *ecumenicity* of the Church, the need for the Russian Church to conform to the general usage of all Orthodox Churches by sacrificing local tradition, even the form of the most conspicuous ritual gesture (the way of making the sign of the Cross) that had been sanctified by the usage of the Fathers. It cannot be denied that this was a great concept, a move toward the Ecumenical Church which would supersede the exclusiveness of the national Church. It is infinitely regrettable that a lack of religious discernment and a disastrous 'externalization' of religion perverted both the ecumenical impulse of the Patriarch Nikon and the heroic conservatism of the Old Believers.

•   •   •

There was a certain charm, sometimes a strange and compelling charm, in this life of the 'old Russian ritualists' (*staro-obryadtsy*), so full, as it was, of naïve archaism. A classic description of their life is found in Melnikov-Pechersky's celebrated epic *In the Forests* (*V lesakh*: 1864), which presents life among the *bezpopovtsy* (sects of Old Believers who were without priests) of the Kostroma district, in the almost virgin forests beyond the Volga, much as it was even as recently as the 1840s and '50s. A modern Russian writer, Grebenchikov (d. 1964), gives another very vivid picture of the *bezpopovtsy* in the distant Altai country, in Siberia, at the beginning of the twentieth century. In these hidden corners of the land the old life, so rigid and formalistic but also imbued with a patriarchal dignity and a certain healthy

---

[11] The text of this petition has been published by Prof. N. Subotin in *Materials for the History of the Raskol* (in Russian), Vol. IV, Moscow, 1878.

moral strictness, as well as picturesque charm, was still preserved almost intact.[12] There exists an even more interesting picture, which I will present here in detail, dating from the '20s of this century, from a time when the Bolsheviks had been in power for ten or twelve years and had suppressed all they could of the old Russian life, brutally destroying millions of family homes, especially those still attached to the ancestral customs. They scattered the members of these families throughout Russia, as well as thousands of members of religious communities. Both the liberty of individual life and the freedom of religion were destroyed. What we are about to describe is a pocket of life on an 'island' surrounded not by open water, but by huge swamps, deep within the immense forest, in an almost inaccessible part of northern Russia at the southern end of the province of Archangel.

This was a community of Old Believers separated from the world by trackless wastes, unknown to the world, a community that had retained all the ritual and family life of seventeenth century Muscovy. Two girls from old, cultivated Russian families, who had been exiled to Archangel, reached this place by following a hazardous trail that had been made known to them. I will let the younger girl speak (whom I knew personally), for she has described this strange journey—leading far back into the past—in a book entitled *On the Shores of the White Sea*.[13] They reached their destination after hours of walking through the swampy forest. 'The path made a sudden turn—a huge, calm lake lay before us, deep blue, with wooded shores. Some canoes were moving on the water. At the edge of the lake there were several houses made of massive logs. Columns of smoke were rising from all the chimneys. In the middle of the hamlet there was a little wooden tower with a bell. When we approached, a very old woman laboriously climbed the steep stairway, and pulled the rope. A long-drawn-out, plaintive, trembling sound echoed across the lake. All the huts opened up at the sound of the bell, and old men and women, as old as Methuselah it seemed, all with a dark leather-bound book in their hands, moved in the direction of a large, low wooden structure behind the tower. We forgot all our tiredness

[12] See the first part of Grebenchikov's novel, *The Churayev Brothers*.
[13] Appeared in German in 1938 (in Paderborn, published by Schoningh), Alexander Anzeruwa, *Am Weissen Meer*.

E

and followed them. It was a church, and we went in. To the right stood bearded old men in black kaftans, to the left were the women. They all wore long dark sarafans,[14] decorated with buttons of gold. Their heads were covered with black scarves. White embroidered sleeves completed their costume. A kind of rosary was wound about the hand of each one present. There were also in the church about a dozen girls and boys. The church was only dimly lighted. On the walls there were dark icons covered over with gilded metal. Wax candles and little oil lamps burned before them. A girl about sixteen or seventeen years old, with long blond hair reaching down to her knees and dressed in a long sarafan, was standing in the middle of the church and reading (almost chanting) from the Psalms, in a limpid, ringing voice, in old Church Slavonic, out of a leather bound book. She was the reader of the community. All those present sung the prayers in unison. The melody was monotonous, sad, almost savage, and had a nasal quality.

'No one turned around when we entered. It was only when the Gospel was about to be read that an old woman approached us and said: "Go out while the words of the Lord are being read. Afterwards you may return." Not until we left the church did we remember how tired we were, and we decided then to go and look for lodging for the night. . . . We began by knocking at the door of a tiny hut set on a lovely site, at the very edge of the lake.

' "Come in, in the name of the Lord," an old trembling voice answered, and we opened the door. The room was in semi-darkness. When our eyes became somewhat accustomed to the gloom, we saw a huge stove, occupying almost half the room. In the middle was a great table, roughly made. A huge bench, well polished and spotless, ran along the wall.

'In the corner a little oil lamp was burning in front of a large image of the Virgin set in a gilded case. The floor was covered with long, narrow, multi-coloured rugs, woven by hand. Two old women were in the room, one seated before a spinning wheel, the other picking over some yellow marsh berries. A whole basket of these berries stood beside her. As we came in, she turned her head.

[14] National costume of Russian women.

' "We would like to spend the night. Do you have any room?" The old woman at the wheel smiled: "We only have this room, and a chicken house. But our neighbours have room. Go there in peace. You can stay there for sure." We thanked them, and went to the neighbours' house. The house was a spacious one, with window shutters of chiselled wood painted in vivid colours. A cow was mooing in the shed. You could hear children's voices. We knocked and went in.

'The room was arranged like that of the old women, but it was much bigger. A large family was gathered round the table. The women were dressed as in church; a little girl perhaps five years old, bare-foot and dressed in a long sarafan with gold buttons, placed a basin full of huckleberries on the table. A steaming fish soup and a pan of fried mushrooms gave off an appetizing smell.

' "You are welcome," a woman of uncertain years said to us in a kindly voice, probably the mother of the many children. She was holding a little boy on her knees. "Sit down and share our supper. Masha, bring some plates." A very pretty girl brought the necessary things. She gave me a smiling look, and I recognized the young reader from the church. I noticed that they had given us special plates, cups and spoons (the Old Believers never eat from dishes that have been used by people of other confessions).

'After supper I looked at the room more closely. Under the icons there were several books on a little table. "Yes, we really do have some good books," the woman said, when she noticed my interest. "We have more of them than in the other houses." We looked at them more closely. Several were in old Church Slavonic and printed in the ancient characters, one was copied by hand, all had thick leather bindings, decorated with golden clasps. There was a Bible, several selections from the works of the Fathers, and some writings of the Old Believers, for example: *Why Must the Sign of the Cross be Made with Two Fingers? The Book on the Direction of Life,* and others of this sort. I came across a popular description of the *Solemn Crowning of the Emperor Nicolas II,* with coloured pictures. It was the only secular book on the table.

' "Have the Bolsheviks done you any harm?" I asked the woman. She laughed: "They know nothing about us, and we hear nothing about them. You can see yourself how hard it is to get here. Not a single Bolshevik has visited us. Here you can go for days through the forests and peat marshes without ever meeting any one, without coming across a single human habitation . . . as far as the Polar Sea. . . . You should have come here for St. Nicolas's Feast—that's when it is beautiful here! The church shines with candlelight, we wear all our holiday clothes—they go back to the time of our grandmother—all brocade. Would you like to see them?"

'At a sign from her mother Masha opened a large chest covered with coloured designs and trimmed with iron bindings, and brought out her own and her mother's holiday dresses. Both of them were of a magnificent black brocade, with great bouquets of silk flowers stitched in gold thread, one a flaming red, the other a bright mauve. Along the hem tiny bells of gold had been fastened, and the front of the dress was decorated with nine magnificently worked golden buttons.

' "Would you like to put it on?" Masha asked me. I put it on over my rumpled and poorly sewn cotton dress, and was trans- formed in an instant. "The nine buttons stand for the nine orders of angels," Masha explained, "the three little ribbons sewn on the shoulders remind you of the Holy Trinity. The four-sided veil, which you put on your head, stands for the four evangelists . . ." and so on. I felt as if I were in a dream or a fairy tale. In the age of Communism, air travel, atheism, chemical discoveries and the electrification of all branches of industry, these people, on the distant shores of their blue lake, were busy explaining the sym- bolic meaning of the buttons on their garments . . .'

A great charm and feeling of peace surrounds this picture of a life regulated and sanctified in all its most minute details by prayer and faith. There is something which attracts the Russian soul, so often tormented, to the strict order of a life governed by religious rite and custom. However an element of psychological instability, an unchecked emotionality, a morbid and passionate, hysterical quality—found sometimes in the Russian soul but quite alien and contrary to the whole spiritual atmosphere and teaching of the Eastern Church—has also, from time to time, entered into the spiritual life of the Russian people—and has manifested itself in peripheral and secondary religious phenomena.

We are reminded in the first place of the ecstatic sects, which were Christian only in external forms, in their vocabulary and some of their theories, being imbued at a deeper level by a thoroughly pagan spirit . . . such sects, for example, as the *Khlysty* and the *Skoptsy* (the Castrates). These sects were not large in numbers. They appeared about the middle of the seventeenth century. Their roots lay in the lower pagan and naturalistic 'strata' of the Russian soul, where obscure and violent passions stirred. The *Khlysty* were morbid and hysterical ecstatics. At their meetings they would form a circle; a rhythm, at first slow and cadenced, would little by little be quickened, becoming in the end turbulent and breath-taking. They would run, stop, clap their hands, gasp and shout; they would scream and pray, and invoke the Holy Spirit. It was the Holy Spirit, so they wrote, who took hold of them like a storm breaking forth, it was an avalanche, a tidal wave, a tempest of fire which carried them away. They were swept up and transported, seized and filled with the divine wind. *Nakatil! Nakatil!*—'He's filled us! He's filled us!' (or 'He's come down! He's come down!')—they would sing, in complete ecstasy.

> Near us a bird is floating,
> He swoops up and comes down.
> O God, O God, O God!
> O Spirit, O Spirit, O Spirit!
> He comes, He comes, He comes!
> Oi Yega, Oi Yega, Oi Yega! [15]
> He's come down, come down!
> The Holy Spirit! The Holy Spirit!
> He goes where He wishes to blow,
> The Holy Spirit! The Holy Spirit!
>
> O, I'm burning, O, I'm burning!
> The Spirit burns, and God burns!
> There's a Light within me, a Light within!
> The Holy Spirit! The Holy Spirit!
> O, I'm burning! I'm burning! I'm burning!
> Spirit! Oi Yega! Oi Yega! Oi Yega! Oi Yega!
> Send! . . . etc., etc.

[15] Exclamations having no definite meaning.

This was almost like a new Dionysian orgy, or the orgies of the great Mother of the Gods in Asia Minor, with their violent motions, or the frenzied dances of the 'whirling Dervishes.' The only Christian element here is the vocabulary. This sect was also profoundly 'antinomian'; it made light of the order in nature and the law of God. It denigrated marriage, and sanctioned an exaggerated and wild asceticism which, following the ecstasies, passed into savage sexual orgies,[16] not unlike certain gnostic sects. This was the old leaven of an ecstatic naturalism going hand in hand with a false and fundamentally anti-Christian spiritualism. This sect developed a fierce hostility toward the Church, which it scorned as 'external' and 'carnal.' The element of chaotic unrestraint, so typical of the Russian soul, sometimes appeared also in forms of religious hysteria among the women of the common people—the *Klikushy* (Screamers)—who made a habit of sobbing and screaming at the most solemn moments of the Liturgy.

These women were quite common in old Russia, especially at the great centres of pilgrimages and in the more famous churches of Moscow, where they would come to be healed.[17] This religious hysteria, completely contrary to the spiritual sobriety inculcated by the Orthodox Church, also had a profound influence on certain aspects of the literary and cultural life of the Russian intelligentsia, on the eve of the First World War. The works of Merezhkovsky, Andrey Bely, certain works of Vyacheslav Ivanov, Bryusov, the young Alexander Blok, and other poets and 'religious philosophers,' bear witness to this. What was being preached was excess, and an orgiastic 'philosophy,' a mixture of paganism and the most sacred Christian mysteries, an ecstasy, a deliberate frenzy, both sensual and at the same time religious, or at least quasi-religious. A smell of decay, an exoticism and morbid emotionality, a quest for sensation, a profound lack of moral equilibrium, seemed to characterize the literature of this period, i.e. the first fifteen years of the twentieth century. These literary circles, while steeped in a refined, worldly and as it were Alexandrian culture, were at the same time, at the subconscious level, connected with the under-

---

[16] Among others, see the famous scenes from the life of the *Khlysty* in the dramatic novel by Melnikov-Pechersky, *On the Mountains.*

[17] On this subject see the interesting work by the psychopathologist, Dr. J. Krainsky, *Klikushy*, Novgorod, 1900 (in Russian).

ground currents of sexualism and pagan mysticism which animated the Russian ecstatic sects, about which we have just been speaking. (This is demonstrated by one of the characteristic works of this literary movement, Bely's *Silver Dove,* which was inspired by the Skoptsy sect.) In spite of its snobbishness and high literary culture, this movement reflected a tendency that was much more closely related to the popular soul than one would have thought at first sight; related, however, to the morbid element of this soul, to its disease, to the sensual and sinister undercurrent which combined the sacred and the scabrous; the most prominent representative of this movement was—at the other end of cultural life—the infamous Rasputin. But, and it must be constantly emphasized, this tendency had nothing to do with the Orthodox Church, or with the truly Christian experience of the Russian people. It was precisely as a safeguard against this spirit that the Church's discipline, and the life in rhythm with her rites and animated by her prayer, were required.

. . .

In spite of the very important role played by the ritual element in the religious life of the Russian people, the conversion of Russia to Christianity was far from being merely the acceptance of an external body of rites and ceremonies. At the time that Christianity was officially introduced into Russia there was, of course, a mass conversion, imposed by the prince of the land. Here is how the chronicler describes the baptism of the people at Kiev: 'Vladimir came down, with the princess's priests and those from Kherson, to the shores of the Dnieper, and an innumerable people gathered and went into the water. Some up to the neck, others up to the chest. Younger ones stood on the bank; men were holding children; adults were standing in the water; and the priests, standing over them, said the prayers.'

But beside this mass conversion, which at first could not fail to be external in many cases, an authentic religious instruction gradually developed, thanks to the enlightened zeal of the princes Vladimir and Yaroslav, and to many missionaries and apostles of the new faith. There was in many cases an inner *shaking of the soul,* for which there is ample testimony even from the earliest times. Indeed Christianity could boast of martyrs at Kiev long before the conversion of Vladimir. His grandmother was a Christian already, and there were Christians among the members of the princes' *druzhiny* from the beginning of the tenth century. These were individual conversions. And Prince Vladimir himself, after his conversion to Christianity, became a new man, a man with a changed heart. The chronicler tells us about this in the following words: 'He listened to Solomon, who said, "He who gives to the poor is giving to God," and other similar passages from Scripture. Having heard this, he commanded all the poor and afflicted to come to the prince's palace and to take all that they needed—to drink, eat, and take sable skins from the prince's treasure house. He gave yet another command, saying, "The weak and the suffering are unable to come to my palace." And so he gave orders to bring carts, and to load them with bread, meat, fish, different kinds of fruit, casks of mead and kvas, and to take them through the city, announcing that where there were sick or poor who could not walk, they were to be given whatever they needed.' His heart had so changed that he did not even wish to inflict capital punishment on highway robbers, something that would not have troubled him at all before his baptism. The bishops even urged him to use this form of punishment. 'Vladimir lived in fear of God; but the number of bandits increased, and the bishops said to Vladimir, "The number of brigands is growing; why not punish them?" And he said to them, "I am afraid to sin. . . ." '

We also have, at the very beginning of this Christian era in Russia, the touching figures of the two young princes and favourite sons of Vladimir, who, after their father's death, let themselves be assassinated by hired men sent by their elder brother Svyatopolk, rather than revolt against him. 'It is not pleasing to God,' the young warrior Boris said when his troops offered him the paternal throne, 'that I should raise my hand against my elder brother; for since my father is dead it is he who must take his place.' The young Russian Church was deeply moved and edified by the way these two young men met death at the hands of their assassins. They were not martyrs giving their life for the faith, and yet they died consciously *for Christ's sake*, they accepted their violent death and their sufferings as a participation in the death of Christ. The ancient author of the story of the murder of the two young princes

—as incorporated in the Chronicle of Nestor—places this prayer on Boris's lips as he faces death, 'Lord Jesus Christ, who hast revealed Thyself on earth in human form for our salvation, and who of Thine own will allowed them to nail Thy hands to the Cross, and didst suffer Thy passion for our sins, give me too the strength to endure. I accept death not from my enemies, but from my brother. O Lord, do not lay this against him as a sin.' It was in the Lord's death, therefore, that this young man found the strength to suffer. In a more detailed version (the *Skazanie,* which dates from the end of the eleventh century) realistic and concrete psychological details abound. The two young brothers are not heroes or representatives of a strict asceticism. It cost them dearly to say farewell to a life so beautiful. Their sadness and inner struggle, especially that of the younger brother Gleb, are painted in a pathetic way. But both find comfort in Christ. After a final prayer—in which he turns to the Saviour with these Pauline words: 'It is for Thy sake that I am crucified all day long, and I am reckoned as a lamb lead to slaughter. Thou knowest, O Lord, that I am not resisting, that I submit'—Boris finds the strength to give himself up to the assassins. He is then a hero of Christian suffering, i.e. of *suffering accepted voluntarily for Christ's sake.* It is indeed in this form, with this central idea of suffering with Christ and for Christ, of suffering accepted in the name of Christ, that the Good News often takes hold of humble souls, and that the religious experience of the great righteous ones and saints of Russia was to bloom and flourish. The Cross of the Lord, suffering accepted voluntarily out of love for Christ—this is what makes the memory of these young princes who were murdered at their brother's command so dear to the Russian people. They were the first saints canonized in Russia. Indeed the Russian Church has invoked them as saints and intercessors before God since 1020, only five years after their death.[18]

Many examples of personal, inner conversions could be cited,

---

[18] On this subject see the fine study by Prof. Fedotov, *The Russian Religious Mind,* Harvard University Press, 1944, pp. 94–110; also Mme. E. Behr Siegel, 'Etudes d'Hagiographies russes,' in the review *Irenikon* (Priory of Amay-sur-Meuse, Vol. XII, 1935).

taken from the first centuries after the official and mass conversion of Russia. There are the celebrated Caves (Crypts) near Kiev, which became the Crypt Monastery (Kievo-Pechersky Monastery), whose first monks were recruited from all classes of the population, and about which the ancient chronicler wrote these eloquent words: 'Many monasteries were founded by kings, boyars and wealthy persons; but they were not as precious as those which were built with tears, fasting, prayers and vigils. Anthony had neither gold nor silver, but he accomplished his task with tears and fasting.'

There is another impressive document: the *Testament* of the Grand Prince Vladimir Monomakh (d. 1125) to his children, filled with a profound Christian spirit which combines wisdom, moderation and justice with the spirit of charity toward others. Many historical tracts show us that an encounter had begun between the soul of the people and the Good News, this suffering and buffeted Russian soul, so often given to orgy and tumult, so imperfect, so full of sins, and not always free from superstition. . . .[19]

---

[19] Here is the way in which the chronicler describes the spiritual state of Russian prisoners carried away by the savage Polovtsy (in 1093), who had been pillaging the country and had seized the town of Torchesk: 'Many Christians were taken. Downhearted, tortured, overwhelmed by hunger and thirst and misery, with pale faces, raw skin, without clothing and barefoot, they were going into a foreign land, their tongues inflamed by thirst, and their feet bruised to the bone. They spoke to one another with tears, saying: "I am from this village. I am from that village." And so they questioned one another with tears—groaning and lifting their eyes to the Most High, who knows the mysteries of the future.'

CHAPTER FOUR

THE DEPTHS OF THE RELIGIOUS LIFE IN THE SOUL OF THE PEOPLE

THE soul has depths in which our decisions first arise or are prepared, decisions which can effect both the physiognomy and the moral destiny of an individual or a people. According to those who believe in a meta-physical, supra-human and divine reality, it is in these depths that spiritual encounters occur and where the soul, for all its unworthiness and frailty, can be made fertile by this encounter and healed of its defects, and receive at least some pale reflection of the Light. Despite the faults and the sins of many representatives of the Russian Church, despite the efforts of the State to subjugate this Church and her sometimes excessive submissiveness to the State, the Russian soul has known and experienced such encounters with God. This is, of course, a general rule of all religious life, and of the Christian life especially. But perhaps because the imperfections of the Russian people were often so evident, or because they themselves have seen them with special clarity and have often *sensed and known that they were sinners,* perhaps for these reasons the encounter of the sinner with the God of mercy (one of the main themes and experiences of Dostoevsky!) lies at the heart of the religious experience of the Russian people, and is its vivifying source. Let me repeat here some of the ideas and intuitions which I have advanced elsewhere.[1]

One of the principal manifestations of the religious element, perhaps its central manifestation, and one of the creative forces which have played and still play an obviously important role in the interior life of the Russian people, is a spiritual state designated in Russian by the term *umilenie,* a word which resists translation. It could perhaps be rendered as 'a sudden softening of the heart,' or 'a flood of deep emotion in the heart.' It is a sudden and unexpected impulse which takes hold of a man, a feeling of

---

[1] In my book *The Spiritual Tradition of Russian Culture* (in Russian), 1959; and in an article in French, 'Quelques traits de l'expérience religieuse russe,' which appeared in *Cahiers de la Nouvelle Epoque,* No. 3, Paris, 1946.

inexplicable tenderness which seizes the hardest of hearts . . . the anguished search for purity and spiritual peace, and the admiration of purity and peace when seen anywhere beyond the self; it is the thrill of love and forgiveness, the tears of repentance and joy, and the gift of self offered in joy. Throughout its thousand year history, in the midst of all its sufferings, sins, weaknesses and faults, the Russian people has always prized this faculty. It appreciated it, it was longing for it, and at times this feeling descended, healing and pacifying the soul. This is why certain particularly 'moving' prayers and hymns in the services of the Orthodox Church have been so loved by the people, and have acted so powerfully upon them in church as they bowed on their face. 'Lord of all powers be with us, for in our adversities we have no protector but thee. . . .' 'Invincible, mysterious and divine power of the holy and life-giving Cross, do not forsake us, sinners that we are. . . .' 'Open unto me the doors of penitence, O Giver of Life. . . .' Such are the moving chants sung, for example, during Lent; or there is the canticle addressed to the Mother of God: 'We have no other help nor any other hope. . . .' And there are many others.

What characterizes this overflowing of the heart is that it is usually also an act of contrition. The abyss of my unworthiness, my weakness, my vices is discovered at the same time that I discover the abyss of divine mercy which has already forgiven me. It is precisely this vast contrast that is experienced as something deeply moving. To put this in theological language, the feeling could be designated as *the encounter between the heart and divine grace, the point of intersection of heart and grace,* the response we give to the action of grace upon our hearts, diseased and crying out to be healed. Yes, it is precisely a response, for in the eyes of the religious conscience grace takes the initiative, it is grace that makes the first move, not us. The stirring thing about all this is, in fact, that God should condescend to us, should receive us in His arms, as the father received his prodigal son, who was as unworthy as we. The undeserved bounty of forgiveness which comes to us from on high, and the feeling of repentance, together form one of the main themes of Christian life in general, a theme manifested with particular force among the Russian people. This people has often felt its sinfulness, and whenever it has been truly religious it has felt with a deep and humble understanding the overwhelming greatness of that grace which brings pardon and renewal. It is indeed the fact of having experienced this feeling himself, and of knowing how to represent it, which raises Dostoevsky (no matter how morbid and hysterical some parts of his work may be) to the level of a true revealer of the soul of the people, and (what is more) of the human soul in general, in its encounter with the divine. In this he is deeply national in the profoundest meaning of this word, as he himself understood it, not because the picture he gives of the Russian people is a precise description from the ethnological viewpoint, but because he reveals what the Russians themselves know to be the source and nourishment of their life at its depths. The conversion which transforms man's interior life suddenly, after a long preparation . . . the action of divine grace on a man's heart, this is one of the great themes to which Dostoevsky returns again and again. Let us recall the story of the duel and then the conversion of the young officer who was to become the *starets* Zossima. Waves of wonderful gentleness flood his soul after his decisive victory over himself, a victory over the old 'I.' 'I almost lost my breath for joy, and my heart felt a gladness that I had never experienced in all my life.' The streams of grace even reach the hardened soul of Raskolnikov, but only after a year and a half of forced labour. His heart is suddenly moved to warmth and love for Sonya, who has followed him to Siberia. 'How it happened he didn't know himself, but suddenly a power threw him at her feet . . . he embraced her knees, weeping. . . . Love revived them, the heart of one holding eternal sources of life for the heart of the other. Love had really revived them, and he felt it deeply in his whole being, which seemed to be born again to a new life.'

In the famous chapter 'Cana in Galilee,' one of the high points in his work, Dostoevsky depicts the overwhelming religious experience of mystical, ineffable gentleness which took hold of Alyosha's soul. 'It was as if threads from all the innumerable worlds created by God were suddenly reunited in his soul, and that it was all aquiver at this encounter with other worlds.' Through the prism of his own individual style as an artist and a psychologist Dostoevsky depicts *spiritual realities,* the authentic experiences of the individual soul, and thus also of the collective soul (since these experiences also have a typical character), as they exist in contact with 'other worlds.'

The theme of the sinner and his conversion, of this healing spiritual upheaval, is something which Dostoevsky felt profoundly to be a personal as well as national theme. He may be described as a painter of sin and grace, of the power of sin and moral depravity but also of the equally astonishing triumph of grace over sin. This theme is of the utmost importance in the soul of the people. Dostoevsky understood that he was touching here the very roots of a nation's spiritual existence. For, as we have said, the decisive moment in the religious outlook or experience of this people (a deeply and truly Christian feature) is the sinner's encounter with the God of mercy and consolation, it is the refuge he finds with God, and the sinner's response to the invitation of grace. This is why the parable of the prodigal son (we may recall the *dukhovny stikh* or popular song on this theme) and the Gospel stories concerning the publicans and sinful women who came to visit Christ find a special echo in the people's soul. This is also what attracts Russians so much to saints who have at one time been brigands or fallen women: Moses Murin (the Ethiopian), and especially Mary of Egypt. The soul of the people has also preserved images of its own past, images either historical or legendary.

> Once there were twelve brigands
> With Kudeyar their ataman . . .

According to popular legend this cruel bandit repented and became a monk on the Solovetsky Islands.

We find the almost epic picture of a repentant bandit in the story of the pilgrim Darya, who was well known to religious circles in St. Petersburg in the middle of the nineteenth century. Returning on foot in winter from a long northern pilgrimage, she fell into the hands of bandits in a forest. They led her to their *izba* and were about to murder her there, before the return of their ataman (chieftain). From this point on I quote the story as told by the old woman herself, and kept in the form of notes by a known St. Petersburg family. It should be noted that 'miserable person' and 'foolish person' are terms which she used in speaking of herself. 'Suddenly there was a silence,' so the old woman continued, 'the silence of death, and the iron hands let the miserable person go. "What are you doing here?" said a low voice in a threatening tone. "Let this old woman alone. What will you gain by beating her to death?" "But we don't want to kill her." "I tell you, leave her alone! Don't touch her!" "What kind of an ataman is this, who will not let us amuse ourselves? Such an ataman . . . why don't we just. . . ." The ataman raised his stick and struck him such a blow on the head that he didn't even let out a cry. "Get rid of this carrion. And don't give me any of your sour looks, or the same thing will happen to you." They went out then, but the miserable person was still out of her mind with terror. Left alone, the ataman suddenly threw himself on his knees before the foolish person, seized her thin legs and began to embrace them, throwing himself on the ground and shedding tears. Then he said: "When I came into the *izba,* they did not hear me, but I saw them : their faces were the faces of wild beasts. I saw you and my soul trembled. I thought I was seeing my own dear mother, standing there, all huddled into the corner. The same little pale face, thin and wrinkled, as when I saw her last. I was rooted to the spot, and shaking, I did not even know myself. I would have let myself be quartered before I'd let them touch you." Then the bandit took me compassionately by the hands, made me sit down on a bench, and began to pull off my dirty boots and wet stockings. He dried my feet with a towel, brought out warm stockings and put them on me, and also some dry shoes, and, still weeping, he repeated: "I am a wretch, and am not worthy of such a happiness. It is as if my mother had risen from the dead, and was letting me take care of her. Oh, my poor little one, how frightened you must have been. Your teeth are still clamped tight like a dead man's. What misery! I have no tea to warm you with. But I will give you some medicine. And he poured something bitter into my mouth out of a bottle. Then he spread out some hay, lay me down on it, took off my coat and covered me, all the while saying: "Don't be afraid of anything, my dear one. I will not let anything evil happen to you. I myself will stand guard over you, and will not close my eyes all night long. Sleep peacefully, as if you were at home, and I will watch over you, rejoicing that God has allowed me to serve you. And forgive me, just as my mother would have done." The morning came, the ataman awakened the old woman while the other bandits were still sleeping, and set her on her way out of the forest. "Forgive me," he said, throwing himself at her feet and embracing them, weeping. "Forgive me for my crimes. Pray to God for me, a poor sinner. I do not dare to beg you to give me a blessing." And I had such pity for him that I fell on his neck and began to sob. For a long time we remained in each other's arms, crying. . . .'

She urged him to repent and to make amends honourably. He replied that it was too late. But this encounter with the old woman did not pass without leaving traces on his soul. She had shaken him deeply. Soon after, he persuaded his comrades to surrender with him to the authorities. 'And they say,' so ends the naïve account of the old woman, 'that these gentlemen were terrified when the bandits, whom they had been unable to catch, appeared on their own before the magistrates. The ataman confessed: "This is the way it is," he said. "I'm the most guilty one of all, I was the one who started everything, don't punish the others too much, I led them astray, they're not responsible. I've earned a greater punishment. All they did was to obey me." The bandits looked at their chieftain and lowered their eyes, some of them fighting back tears. They say that all the bandits got a light punishment for having confessed.' [2]

Even in common life in Russia in the last century, and also in the literature which reflects this life, this theme is often found: the guilty one freely gives himself up, under the impulse of a religious conscience, into the hands of justice, openly confesses his crimes before an assembly of the people, and before the eyes of all makes an act of profound and sudden repentance. Dostoevsky and Tolstoy understood the deeply moving character of this public repentance, of this deep contrition of the criminal who had no desire to spare himself, who would stop at nothing to efface his fault and receive his due punishment. Remember the scene from Tolstoy's 'The Power of Darkness,' when Nikita freely confesses

[2] Published in the review *Domashnaya Beseda,* 1864.

his crime before the gathered people, while the stammering Akim, his father, representing the voice of his son's conscience, urges the village militia to be patient and give the criminal a chance to clear his conscience by this act of public contrition: 'Hold on, before you draw up your report of the testimony! Shut up for a bit! God's work is being done here. A man is confessing his crime before God.' And, at the end of the scene, he shouts with enthusiasm: 'God will forgive you, my dear son! You have had no pity on yourself, and now it is God who will have pity on you. It is God . . . it is God. . . .'

In the same way, in another moving, sombre drama, taken from rural life—'A Bitter Fate' by Pisemsky—we see the hero, the proud, magnificent peasant Anany, voluntarily surrendering to the authorities, not wishing to lighten his responsibility by making others share it: 'My sin is the greatest of all, and I have no desire to lighten my punishment. Only may God help me to bear it patiently. Even the torments of death I will accept willingly, that I may obtain forgiveness of my great crime.'

These two contrasting poles in the Russian soul: the depth of moral fall and the spontaneous effort to right the wrong, have been presented—as we have seen—in Dostoevsky's *Diary of a Writer*. It is clear that in this realm of the spiritual life what the believer sees as the action of grace cannot be limited to the moral experience of one people, or even of one Church. There can be no question of a monopoly on the fruits of grace. How many souls have been reawakened by the unexpected force of inner cleansing, the floods of tenderness and contrition, by spiritual illumination, not only among all Christians but also in general among all people who are seeking God. And yet perhaps few people have felt their own weakness, their own moral unworthiness in the face of life-giving grace, as vividly as the Russian people.

• • •

This overflowing tenderness that takes hold of the soul of the repentant sinner, the deep emotion of prayer, the tears of contrition and joy at the feet of the merciful Lord—this is what has given strength to the soul of the Russian people in the midst of all its weaknesses and falls, and in spite of them. Often this is inseparable from the need to feel the *nearness of God* in the midst

81

of this sinful world. This explains, for example, the great influence exercised on the widest range of people by the holy men of spiritually illumined life—the *startsy* (elders). It also explains the flood of pilgrims, moving from one holy place to another—already mentioned in the first chapter—who travelled across Russia from the far north to the southern borders with extraordinary endurance and enterprise, right down to the beginning of the twentieth century. This too explains the great importance which miraculous icons have had in the life of the people. The writer Gleb Uspensky, who belonged really to the Russian radical intelligentsia but was, nevertheless, well acquainted with the popular soul and a man filled with a lively concern for the spiritual welfare of the people, has given us an acute and objective description of the annual transfer of the celebrated icon of the Holy Mother of Tikhvin. In the words of a rough peasant.·. . .

'. . . our most Holy Mother was brought out of the church, the archimandrites bowing deeply and taking leave of one another at the monastery door, and the people took over the carrying of the icon. All of them—from Tikhvin and from Staraya Russa—were inspired as one man. And the people kept on coming and coming by the thousands—from all the villages and cities. At the entrance to each village the clergy would come to meet the icon with banners flying, and they would carry it into the church. They carried her high, our Most Holy One, high above the crowd, and she gleamed in the sun like a bright fire. . . . Women, especially nuns, they came from all over, singing on and on like the angels of heaven—Oh! How fine it was to hear "Thou who dost intercede for us." The singing never stopped for a minute, day or night. A huge crowd walked along and sang. And there was plenty of everything, just like a miracle. Who gave this crowd something to eat and drink? She did it; the Queen of mercy. If it was a field where they stopped, great fires were suddenly lit up, huge cook-pots steamed on the fires, all kinds of food was cooked, every one ate his fill, and drank, and every one was happy and satisfied. And the singing went on night and day around the icon, a great crowd of people was always around it, and she was carried along the whole long road in the arms of the people. There wasn't a single one left of all those poor hoboes you see so much of on the highways. Every one found food, and work, and lodging, thanks to the Holy Virgin.'

For the soul of the people these holy icons are a point of contact with the world of divine realities; in these icons the nearness of condescending and merciful grace becomes palpable, so to speak. The greatest of the epic painters of the life of the Russian people, Leo Tolstoy, inserted in one of the scenes in *War and Peace* the Te Deum which the Russian troops sang on the eve of the battle of Borodino, before the image of the Holy Mother of Smolensk:

'A procession was following, coming up the road from the village of Borodino. At the head of the column there was the infantry, in perfect order, their shakos in their hands and their rifles lowered, advancing along the dusty road. Behind the infantry a religious chant could be heard. Going ahead of Pierre, the soldiers and militia ran to meet it. "They are carrying the Holy Mother, the merciful One, the Holy Mother of Iberia. . . ." ". . . the Holy Mother of Smolensk," another corrected. The militiamen from the village as well as those who were working on the gun position threw down their spades and ran in front of the procession. Behind the battalion of infantry walked the clergy—an old priest with a *kamilavka* [3] on his head, and other ecclesiastics and the choir following. Behind them, soldiers and officers were carrying a large icon that had been brought out of the ruins of Smolensk, and had since then followed the army everywhere it went. Groups of soldiers came up and ran around it on all sides, crowding up to it, bowing to the ground, their heads uncovered.

'Pierre's whole attention was caught by the serious expression on the faces of the soldiers and militiamen, who were all looking at the icon with the same rapt intensity. As soon as the tired singers (this was the twentieth Te Deum they had sung that day) began to intone in a monotonous and mechanical way "Protect thy servants against all evils, O Mother of God," and the priest and deacon joined in the chant and continued "for we flee to thee as to a firm defence, as to One who intercedes for us with the Lord"—the same consciousness of the solemn significance of this moment illuminated all faces, the same expression Pierre had already encountered on many faces during the course of the day. The heads

[3] A kind of cylindrical velvet hat worn by Orthodox archpriests.

bowed down with increasing fervour. Groans could be heard, and the sound of hands beating on chests as they made the sign of the Cross. . . .'

In numerous great crises in Russian history there have been interventions of miraculous icons of the Virgin—the Holy Mother of the Don accompanied the Russian troops on the battlefield of Kulikovo, where the Tatar forces were overthrown; the Holy Mother of Kasan accompanied the troops of Minin and Pozharsky when they liberated Moscow from the Poles in 1613.[4]

Thus too in the famous church of the Holy Mother of Iberia in Moscow the soul of the people used to come to pour out and bewail its afflictions before God. Ivan Kireevsky, the great religious philosopher and one of the fathers of the Slavophile movement, describes in the following way the impression made upon him as the people prayed before this deeply venerated icon: 'One day I was in the church and looking at the miraculous icon of the Holy Mother, meditating on the child-like faith of the people who were praying before it. Several women and sick old men were kneeling and bowing down to the ground and making the sign of the Cross. With a lively faith I looked at the holy features of the icon, and I began to understand the mystery of this miraculous power. No, this was not a simple board with an image on it. For whole centuries it had absorbed the torrents of prayers which have poured over it, the cries of afflicted and unhappy souls. It has therefore been filled with this power of faith, which now shines from it in order to be reflected in the hearts of these supplicants. It has become a living organ, a point of contact between man and the Creator. As I thought about all this, I once more looked at the old men and women with their children, bowing humbly, and looked too at the holy icon. And I saw the features of the Mother of God take on life. She was looking at these poor people with love and pity. . . . I knelt down there, and prayed humbly before her.' [5]

How many mothers and brides came here in sorrow to pray for their children or husbands during the First World War and the

[4] cf. Count Bennigsen, 'Les Icônes de L'Eglise russe,' in *Irenikon*, May–June, 1928, p. 248.
[5] Quoted by Herzen, *My Past and Thoughts*, Vol. 2.

terrible time of the civil war that followed? How the popular soul used to pray too before the relics of St. Sergius in the monastery of the Trinity. These silent cries, these passionate appeals from the masses of people, before the face of God. How typical they are! How they draw us into the interior of the soul of the people, as it was only forty years ago! And again now, for in the midst of all the current religious persecution, people are once more streaming from all parts of Russia to the shrine of St. Sergius.

.   .   .

The love of *religious or cultic beauty*, so deep-rooted in the popular soul, may also be explained in large part by this over-flowing of emotion before the boundless condescension of God. The aesthetic charm of the cult and of the whole atmosphere of the church had a profound effect on the distant ancestors of present-day Russians. The story of the conversion of St. Vladimir, toward the end of the tenth century, bears witness to this. According to the legend Vladimir had sent emissaries to different lands in order to find the best religion. They came to the Volga Bulgarians (who were Muslims) and saw their cult, 'but there was nothing joyous about it; on the contrary, everything there was sad and gloomy, and their religion was not good.' What they saw among the Germans pleased them no more. 'We came to the Germans and saw them worship at length in their churches, but we saw no beauty there.' They went then to the Greeks, and the Greeks took them to the place where they worshipped their God. 'And we did not know if we were in heaven or on earth, for on earth there is no such beauty. Nor do we know what we ought to say. One thing only do we know: that God was living there with men, and that their form of worship is the best of all. We cannot forget this beauty. Just as a man refuses to eat what is bitter after having tasted what is sweet, so we cannot remain with you here.'

The ancient documents of Russian history are full of moving descriptions of this cultic beauty. Thus in the middle of the eleventh century, in a sermon commemorating the late Prince Vladimir, Metropolitan Ilarion says: 'Behold the city gleaming in majesty, behold the churches flourishing, behold the Christian faith increasing, see how the city is sanctified by the holy icons, illuminated, perfumed with incense and resounding with hymns of praise and divine canticles. . . .' A thrill of enthusiasm can be felt running through the chronicler's tale when he speaks of the construction, by Prince Andrey Bogolubsky (in 1159) of the celebrated Cathedral of the Assumption in Vladimir. This was a temple 'such as never has been in Russia and never will be. The most pious Prince Andrey is to be compared with King Solomon. He erected a cathedral of beauty in Vladimir, he decorated it with gold, silver, precious stones and pearls, and made it magnificent with mosaics and bas-reliefs. He had the domes and the great entrance doors gilded, he made it like the temple of Solomon in its splendour.' A series of old texts, especially from the fifteenth century on, speak with enthusiasm of the beauty of the cult, and of the flashing blaze of countless church domes throughout the whole Russian land. Thus in one of the variations of the story of the Council of Florence, dating from the fifteenth century, we find the following words addressed to the Grand Duke Basil the Blind : 'It is right that you should rejoice with all the people in the true Orthodox faith, which shines throughout the world. The grace of God is upon us as a shining mantle, and the churches of God are as flowers, as the stars of the sky, as the gleaming rays of the sun, magnificently adorned, and resounding with holy songs.' [6]

Cultic beauty became one of the sources of Russia's national consciousness, one of the constituent elements in the concept of 'Holy Russia.' [7] This love of cultic beauty has remained as one of the distinctive characteristics of popular Russian psychology throughout the centuries. It is often in these external forms of liturgical beauty that the soul of the people feels itself seized by an inexpressible Presence. Here is a recent incident, which I heard about from an eye witness. At the beginning of the German-Russian war, in 1941, an Orthodox Liturgy was authorized by the Germans in a camp of Russian prisoners not far from St. Petersburg. Almost all the Russian war prisoners expressed the desire to be present—most of them probably out of curiosity. A native of the Baltic districts who is an acquaintance of mine, whom the

<hr/>

[6] Quoted by A. Popov, *Istoriko-Literaturny obzor polem. literatury*, 1875, p. 395.
[7] See the remarkable article by Prof. A. Solovyov, 'Holy Russia,' in *Zbornik russkago archelog. obshestva v korolevstve S.H.S.*, Belgrade, 1927, Vol. I.

Germans had seized and compelled to act as an interpreter, was also there. Not far from him there stood a young Russian peasant, about 18 years old, a prisoner of war who since infancy had had no opportunity to see the cult of the Church. The Orthodox priest of the village church (which the Germans had just reopened) celebrated the Liturgy with feeling, in the open air. There was snow on the ground. A little choir of five women who had come from the village with the priest sang the responses and the canticles. Suddenly this lad exclaimed in an undertone: 'My God, how beautiful that is.' His heart had been touched by this liturgical beauty. This is one of the paths along which grace encounters the soul of the people.

Let us recall, also, this typical passage from an old Russian text of *The Legend of Peter, Son of the Tartar King*. 'Now this young man came with the Bishop of Rostov and saw the church all decorated with gold, pearls and precious stones, decked like a bride, and heard harmonious chanting—one choir in the church of the Holy Mother was singing in the Greek tongue, the other in Russian. Having seen and heard all this, the young man felt a fire kindled in his heart, and though he was not of the true faith his soul was illumined by the ways of the divine sun, and he fell at the feet of the holy bishop.' In the Russian prison camp there was no gold, nor pearls, nor gems, nor choirs singing antiphonally, but the beauty of the cult was present, even under the most austere external conditions, and it had 'melted' this young man's soul.

The very words of the Church's hymns, which with the liturgical melodies are often known by heart, were also full of great spiritual beauty for the religious mind, and profoundly 'moving.' The great writer Chekhov has described this for us with keen perception and love in his well-known story 'Holy Night.' You will recall how the monk Heironymus is operating the ferry which is carrying pilgrims from one bank of the river to the other on Easter night, and how he speaks of his best friend, the Heirodeacon Nicolas, who had just died, and who used to write such fine 'akathists' or poems of religious praise. 'Now it is a great gift to know how to compose akathists. . . . They must be written in such a way that the one who is praying will rejoice and weep in his heart, that he will shudder, and be seized by a spirit of reverence. In the poem of praise dedicated to the Mother of God, there are these words: "Hail, O Highness inaccessible to the thought of men! Hail, O Depth unfathomable even for the sight of angels!" And in another place in this same hymn it is said: "Hail, Tree of shining fruit which nourish the faithful. Hail, Tree whose leaves are a blessed shelter and by whom many are defended." Heironymus was as it were suddenly frightened by something, and intimidated, and covered his face with his hands and shook his head. "Tree of shining fruit, Tree whose leaves are a blessed shelter . . ." he murmured, "You have to be a real expert to find such words. You must have a special gift from God!" '

This impulsive feeling for liturgical beauty, for religious beauty, is revealed too in the phenomenon of pilgrimage so intimately connected with these aspirations of the soul of the people. The pilgrims speak enthusiastically of the magnificence, the moving beauty of the divine services they attend. Here is the testimony of the monk Parthen. The story of his pilgrimage to Mt. Athos in the '30s of the last century was one of Dostoevsky's favourite books. Some of the features of his starets Zossima were inspired by this figure. With profound emotion the naïve and pious monk tells of one of his first impressions of Mt. Athos—the solemn Vespers in the Monastery of Hilendar. 'Truly this Vespers was a blessing for me. It was the first time that I had seen a service of such beauty. When I was in the church I really felt as if I were in heaven, so filled was I with dread and joy.' Everything that he saw amazed him. 'The beauty of the ancient icons on the great iconostas, the mosaics and slabs of coloured marble . . .' After the service he returned to the monastery quarters where his travelling companion was waiting for him. His companion asked him what he had seen, and he answered: 'I can't tell you whether I was on earth or in heaven. I have never seen or heard anything to compare with what I have just seen and heard, nor can I express it to you. . . . There is only one thing I can say: Happy are we to have come here. . . .' This naïve story reminds us a little of the words of Prince Vladimir's envoys. The fact that popular religious experience was strongly impregnated with aesthetic elements carried with it, however, some genuine spiritual dangers. We have already spoken of this in the preceding chapter. The religious feeling could become shallow and attached primarily to the forms of the cult, and this could at times give rise to an excessive and intolerant ritualism.

· · ·

And yet liturgical beauty serves only to indicate the nearness of another world—the divine world that is so far superior to ours and is filled with an overpowering Presence. Beauty serves only to prepare the soul for this encounter with God. Thus it is the nearness of the Divine, the contemplation of heavenly beauty and of one's own unworthiness which has inspired this moving canticle sung during Holy Week: 'I behold, O my Lord, Thy banquet chamber magnificently arrayed, but I have no garment to put on that I might enter in. . . .'

It is especially in the Sacrament of Holy Communion, the Sacrament of God's boundless condescension, that the presence of God Most Holy is revealed to the believer's heart with incomparable power, and also the sense of his own littleness and unworthiness in the face of God. We have already spoken of this, and will dwell on it again here only for a moment. The soul is shaken by the grandeur of this experience: the coming of the Lord and His presence in the midst of the faithful. Here the King of kings, the Master of all Creation, the Living Lord, He who suffered and was glorified, is present in the midst of us, in all His Glory, surrounded by the Heavenly Powers. 'For this is the King of Glory who comes in, this is that which has been accomplished by the mysterious Sacrifice.' 'We who represent in a mysterious way the cherubim—let us now lay aside all earthly thoughts, that we may receive the Lord of All.'

This magnificent Liturgy of the Orthodox Church and the holiness of the Eucharistic mystery have spoken to the Russian religious soul, and have profoundly influenced it, have nourished the spiritual life of Russia's holy and righteous men. In a letter to Prince Andrey of Mozhaysk (1408–13) St. Cyril of Belo-ozero once wrote: 'My Lord, conduct yourself in church with fear and reverence, as if you were in heaven, for the church is called "heaven on earth," because the Sacraments of Christ are celebrated there.' St. Sergius of Radonezh, his spiritual master and one of the great Russian saints, had the gift of special fervour in the Eucharist. In the account of his life written by his disciple Epiphan we are told that he was seen surrounded by celestial fire as he celebrated the Holy Eucharist.

The Lord comes and enters our souls, as they tremble in their depths and lie prostrate before Him. 'Lord, I am not worthy to come near, I am not worthy to contemplate Thy heavenly summits, but I take courage and commit myself to Thy mercy, I flee unto Thee.' 'I am not worthy that Thou shouldst come under the roof of my soul, for it is all in ruins, and there is no place in me worthy enough for Thee to lay Thy head. But come! Enlighten and heal my darkened thoughts, my afflicted soul.' These words from the ancient Eucharistic prayers—from the prayers of St. John Chrysostom, St. Basil, St. Ephraim and other Fathers of the Eastern Church—find their echo in the soul of the Russian believer. Here is the way in which a great Russian saint, Dimitry of Rostov (a contemporary of Peter the Great), expressed the joy of the Eucharistic union or encounter with God: 'Enter, O Light, and enlighten my darkness! Enter, O Life, and enliven my soul, which is spiritually dead. Enter, O my Healer, and heal my sores! Enter, O Fire Divine, consume the thorns of my sins and enkindle my heart with the flame of Thy love! Enter, O my King, and take Thy place upon the throne of my heart, and reign over it, for Thou alone art my King and Saviour!' And after receiving the Sacrament: 'O Exaltation of my soul, O joy of my spirit and Balm of my heart, O merciful Jesus—do Thou remain with me always, and by Thine almighty hand keep me with Thee and in Thee. Let me be united to Thee in one spirit and let all my thoughts and all my words and all my acts be in Thee, for Thee, and by Thee, for without Thee I can do nothing. Henceforth let me live no longer for myself, but for Thee, my Lord and Benefactor. Let all the feelings, all the motions of my soul and body be henceforth not in the service of self, but in Thy service, my Creator, that I may live and move in Thee, and let all the powers of my soul and body be subject to Thee, O my Saviour, and let my whole life, until my dying breath, be consecrated to the glory of Thy Holy Name, O my God. Amen.' It was near the beginning of the century that a great Russian layman, an ardent Christian and an eminent religious thinker, spoke these words as he lay on the point of death: 'The royal doors are opening! The great Liturgy is about to begin.' [8]

. . .

A compassion and pity for one's neighbour, inspired by the Gospel, have sown many seeds in the soul of the people, have put down many roots there, and have often influenced it at its very depths. A boundless pity and uncalculating mercy are, as we shall see, striking features of the great just men and saints of Russia. The same unlimited and uncalculating pity is also found, in spontaneous but fleeting gleams, in the soul of the Russian people, touched by the Good News.

This popular soul has often demonstrated a great natural goodness alongside fits of cruelty, which bursts out at times in an elemental way and then passes—as in the bloody uprisings which fill Russian history. (We may recall the savage uprising of 1648, at the beginning of the reign of Alexis Mikhailovich, with its repulsive cruelty, or the tragic rebellions of Stenka Razin and Pugachev, which had, incidentally, strong social implications.) There is a great good-naturedness in the Russian people, a good nature often mixed with indifference, with a certain nonchalance, and yet a sympathetic nonchalance, for it is full of tolerance and a friendly understanding of one's neighbour, with all his sins and faults. No one, after all, is perfect. We are speaking here, however, of something more than this facile and tolerant good-naturedness—which characterizes the Russian people but is really something lying on the very surface of the moral life. The Good News has often taken root in the most hidden recesses of the soul of the people, half-consciously or subconsciously, implanting there an *active, true compassion,* shown for example toward those who have been cast out by society : criminals condemned to forced labour, prisoners, a conquered and suffering enemy. Dostoevsky drew attention to this striking characteristic of the Russian soul—having had occasion to observe it when he was himself a convict. Criminals justly condemned for their crimes by the law were referred to as 'poor unfortunates' (*neschastnenkye*) in the language of the common people. The crime was not excused; Dostoevsky demonstrates this to us in a clear and convincing way in his *Diary*

---

[8] The central doors of the iconostasis which separate the altar from the rest of the church. These were the dying words of the religious philosopher, Prince Eugene Trubetskoy, 1863–1920.

of a Writer and other places; but once discovered and condemned, the criminal became a brother fallen into misfortune. One of the characteristic and most attractive features of the influence of the Christian message on the moral ideal of old Russia was the visiting of prisoners by highly placed persons—by the Tsar himself—at the great feasts of the Christian year, especially during Holy Week. This became part of the 'ritual' of the life of the Tsars in the seventeenth century. Tsar Alexis Mikhailovich in particular showed a personal and active kindness in his observation of this pious custom—we are told by the great Russian historian Platonov.[9] As he visited the prisons and hospitals he would distribute large sums of money, often freeing those held in prison, paying off unrepayable debts, and helping the poor and the sick.

One concept which marked the medieval period in the West and also left a deep imprint on the people of Russia was the idea that *Christ is with us* in the guise of a beggar, and accepts our alms and acts of charity in this way.[10] This was a concept, or rather a real and overwhelming *experience,* which gave rise to many pious legends.[11] It also made the words of Matt. 25 ring in the hearts of believers, and does so down to the present day.

Prince Andrey Bogolyubsky would always give a beggar what he wanted, and never refused a beggar's request, reflecting that 'it is perhaps Christ who has come to test me.' [12] The Metropolitan of Kiev, Ivan IV, would say to each bishop he consecrated: 'My son, turn to almsgiving. Behold Christ hidden in the rags of the beggar, and stretch out your hand.' We find these same ideas in the final instructions which St. Nikon of Radonezh (disciple and successor of St. Sergius) gave to the monks of his monastery just before his death. We find them also in the monastic Ordo of St. Euphrosin of Pskov.[13] This is a peculiarly Christian experience, but common, as I have said, to the East and the West.

[9] S. Platonov, *Lektsii po russkoy istorii,* Petrograd, 1917, p. 408.

[10] Let us recall, for example, the legend of the pious Count Thibaud of Champagne and the leper (in Caesarius Heisterbacensis, *Dialogus miraculorum,* Hist. VIII, cap. 31), the story of St. Francis of Assisi and the leper (Celano, *Legenda Secunda,* Cap. V) and other similar legends; cf. my article 'The Image of the Suffering Christ in the Religious Experience of the Middle Ages' (in Russian) in *Trudy russkikh uchenikh za granitsey,* Berlin, 1923, Vol. II.

[11] For example the legend entitled *O nekoem igumenie,* in a manuscript collection of monastic legends; cf. S. Smirnov, *Kak sluzhili miru · podvizhniki-drevney,* 1903, pp. 77–8.

[12] See the chronicle *Ipatievskaya Letopis,* p. 397.

THE RELIGIOUS LIFE

From conversations I have had with young Russian war prisoners and workers deported to Western Europe during the last war, I have had repeated proof that it is especially the words of Matt. 25 which have impressed those who have shown any interest in questions of religion. 'I was hungry and you fed me, I was sick and in prison and you visited me . . . and each time you have done so to one of the least of my brethren, you have done it to me.'

Here is a story which I heard from a friend, a young Pole taken by the Germans and compelled to serve as an interpreter on the Russian front (he was able to escape later). In the first winter of the Russian campaign, during a terrible cold spell (there were 35 degrees of frost), he found himself in a car with a young German officer, driving along a highway. Both of them were completely numb with cold. They decided to stop at the first cottage of the first village they came to in order to warm up. The cottage which the two young men chanced to enter was one of the poorest in the village, without any wooden floor. It was swarming with children. The family living there had in fact given shelter to two families from a neighbouring village that had been burned by the Germans as they retreated. A harsh order had been given to burn all the villages through which the German troops were retreating, that the enemy might find nothing but ruin in its way. This was a virtual death sentence for the poor people who were the brunt of this cruel order, and who, in the 35 degree weather, were left with no shelter even for their children. One of these two families had been able to rescue a cow, the other had saved a sack of meal. This was all they had been able to carry away. As the two young men came in a young woman in the cottage began to pour out her heart in the Russian manner, as village women do, making her complaint in a half-lyrical recital (*prichitanya*): 'The times are hard, and everything goes so badly, and you suffer, and it's so bitterly cold . . .' and so on. And then, turning to the two young men (one Polish and the other German, although she took both of them for Germans) she began to complain to them. 'It is no longer gay for you either. You are here in a strange land, in this cold weather. Ah, you are so young, and so far from your families!' Then she left the room, and returned a few minutes later with a

[13] cf. Smirnov, p. 77.

93

jug of hot milk and two large chunks of bread, and gave them to the two men. When they began to resist, she insisted—it would do them good to drink something hot and eat a little. And this was the woman whose house had been deliberately burned down by the Germans the day before, in the neighbouring village. The two young men were overwhelmed. This had nothing at all to do with the preaching of hatred between nations, races or classes. This was a different message: the seeds of the Good News had fallen deep into the subconsciousness of these people. This was an application in life of the Gospel message, by a simple village woman who was probably not even aware of what she was doing.

There is in the fabric of classic Russian literature an element of continuity which runs through it like a bright thread and secretly unifies the whole. The words of the great poet Pushkin could be inscribed as an epigraph for this literature: 'Pity for the fallen I required—*I milost k padshim prizvyal.*' The whole of Russian literature is marked by this sign: by respect for the person of the other . . . for his human dignity, for his rights. This whole literature breathes compassion and pity for the suffering man, without respect to class, position, culture or nationality. All the great Russian classics are at times convulsed by a shudder of pity. They uphold pity and respect for human dignity, for human personality as such, and especially when this personality is denigrated and trampled under foot. They uphold this compassion and respect by means of images taken from life as it really is. In this connection Dostoevsky is only the most eloquent of all the great masters of Russian literature. When he appeals to our pity he is the one who speaks for them all, as in such works as *The Insulted and the Injured, Poor Folk, The House of Death.* Dostoevsky's work is profoundly national and at the same time profoundly Christian. This is the seed of the Good News received by the Russian people in the depths of its subconscious, and at times it has brought forth a rich harvest. I do not mean to idealize: there have been in the past and there still are now many harsh and negative traits in the Russian character. But whenever and wherever the seed of the Gospel has germinated, it has manifested itself in this compassion for the unfortunate, for the fallen, for the poor in spirit, even for the guilty, and criminals. We shall see that this is one of the most important features of the spiritual physiognomy of the great just men and saints of Russia: the condescension of the God-made-Man preached not by words, but by a charity shown to the sinner, to the one who is abandoned and rejected by all, *even to the enemy fallen and lying stretched out on the ground.* (A Russian proverb that has been forgotten in our time says: 'You don't rain blows on a man when he is down.') *This divine condescension can be preached effectively only by personal example.* It was the great just men and saints who really understood this. But the Russian people as a whole has heard this message too, *and at times it has heeded it.* And its ethical ideal (to which it has been so often unfaithful) was in times past—and perhaps not only in the past—the ideal of mercy and pity. It had need of pity and compassion itself, and knew something of what it means. It is really only when pity has been received that it is given.

I should like to quote here these words of Dostoevsky, words that are as Russian (in the good sense of the term, for there are also some ugly things which are very Russian) as they are Christian: 'What happiness can exist that is founded on another's misfortune? Imagine that you are in the process of building the edifice of human destiny with a view to making men happy in the end, finally bestowing upon them peace and repose. And then imagine that in order to attain this end it is necessary, absolutely indispensable, that you make *one* single human being die in torment; even grant that this is a being who does not seem very worthy in our eyes, who might even, from a certain point of view, seem to be ridiculous. Then all that's required is to cover him with shame and insult, and let him die in torment, and then erect your building on the tears of this dishonoured man. Do you consent to be the architect of such a building, on this condition? That's the problem. And could you admit, even for an instant, the idea that the men for whom this edifice was built could, in turn, accept such happiness at your hands, founded on the suffering of a human being (even the most miserable wretch) put to death in a cruel and unjust way? Would they, having accepted this happiness, be able to remain happy?' [14]

[14] Dostoevsky's famous speech on Pushkin in 1880, published in his *Diary of a Writer.*

I would like also to note a few instances of magnanimity toward the conquered enemy that have been inspired, surely, by the message of the Gospel. It goes without saying that throughout the political history of Russia—as with all nations—there are many acts of violence and injustice. But alongside these there are also shining acts of magnanimity, on the international level, profoundly Christian in their inspiration. Let us recall the conduct of Alexander I in Paris in 1814. He came not as a conqueror but as a liberator and friend of the French people. Before the eyes of Europe he showed how he meant to avenge the fall of Moscow. Paris was not burned. And on March 29th (April 10th), 1814, on the Place de la Révolution (now the Place de la Concorde), at the very place where Louis XVI had been guillotined, there was a celebration of the Eastern Church's magnificent service of Easter night, so full of joy and the message of reconciliation ('Let us embrace one another, and forgive one another our offences: for Christ is risen from the dead!')—as a service of expiation and reconciliation, with the Russian troops drawn up in dress uniform. This was his revenge for Moscow, as he remarked explicitly on his return to St. Petersburg to his close friend Prince Alexander Golitsin.[15] He had drawn here from the depths of Christian experience which sometimes take hold of the soul of the Russian people, at all levels of the social scale. The magnanimous conduct of the Emperor Alexander I toward his conquered enemy increased the admiration which he inspired among people in all levels of Russian Society.[16] As in the patriotic war of 1812, he acted here as the true representative of his people, of their noblest impulses. The nation had been profoundly shaken by the terrible war, and by the unexpected rescue at the brink of the precipice. The people and the Tsar unanimously attributed this deliverance not to their own merits or feats of strength, but to the mercy of God. So then, those who had been saved in an amazing and unexpected manner were inspired to recognize the author of their salvation, and to pardon their vanquished and suffering enemy.

The Russian religious thinker Peter Chaadayev, himself a veteran

---

[15] Prince A. Golitsin's story has been published in the review *Russky Arkhiv*, 1886, Vol. II, p. 97.
[16] cf. the poem of the young Pushkin, written when he was 15 years of age: *Recollections of Tsarskoe-Selo.*

of the war of 1812-14, shared the religious attitude of the Emperor Alexander. In 1835 he wrote (to A. N. Turgenev): 'Why should I not have the right to say that Russia is too powerful to conduct her political affairs like other nations, that her vocation in the world is the political leadership of all humanity, that Emperor Alexander I understood this perfectly, and that this was his greatest glory; that Providence has made us too great to be egoists, that it has placed us outside national interests and laid upon us the concern for mankind? Russia, if she understands her vocation, ought to take the initiative in realizing all religious ideas, for she does not have the attachments, the passions, the ideas and interests of Europe.' [17]

Fine words! Does Russia to-day understand them? They can be understood only to the extent that Russians are rooted in Christian *humility*, in the sense of responsibility before God, and of the Christian *solidarity* of all people in full mutual compassion, including the suffering and conquered enemy. This Christian solidarity of all peoples was proclaimed by Dostoevsky with prophetic inspiration in a speech he delivered at the unveiling of the monument to Pushkin in Moscow in 1880. This brotherhood of people *in Christ* is also an idea to which Khomyakov, one of the greatest Russian religious thinkers, returns again and again in his religious and patriotic poetry.

On an even higher plane, in the personalities of the great Russian saints, we shall see this attitude increase in power and depth, and penetrate the whole fabric of life.

. . .

To close this sketch of the depths of the Russian soul as influenced by Christian teaching and experience, I would like to take note of one further characteristic: *simplicity of heart*. We shall see its full importance among the saints and righteous men. In the soul of the people there was—alongside the inclination to hysteria and excessiveness already mentioned—an often naïve and primitive simplicity. And yet in this 'primitive' simplicity of the common people vistas and depths may often be seen which are not apparent at first glance, the signs of a spiritual authenticity

[17] Works and letters of P. J. Chaadayev, published by M. Gershenson, Vol. I, Moscow, 1913, p. 185.

G

nourished by contact with the Gospel.[18] In radical contrast to the morbid hysteria which could often be found and of which we have already given so many examples, *the main stream of popular Russian piety, its ideal, remains imbued with this simplicity,* so characteristic of the teaching and spirit of the Gospel, and of the Orthodox Church.

Among the majority of great Russian writers (not in Dostoevsky, however)[19] there is a tendency which can be connected with this national character: the cult of sober simplicity. It is this, among other things, which constitutes the charm of the style and whole aesthetic outlook of Pushkin—the greatest of Russian poets. A cult of true simplicity, clear and beautiful, full of feeling, at times full of deep passion; and yet this feeling is subdued or reserved in its expression and the passion is dominated. The ring of authenticity is all the greater, then, all the more poignant. The depth is often stormy and turbulent, but here is a passion illumined by beauty, an impetuousness mastered and tamed, even transfigured, so to speak, by a creative movement, by a breath of hidden spirituality. On the 'psychic' plane this was already a certain anticipation of the spiritual life, a presentiment of the creative, calming and transfiguring power of the Spirit as manifested in beauty—a religious awareness partly unrecognized by the poet himself, who remained torn by inner conflicts.

Pushkin and the other great classic authors of Russia, especially Leo Tolstoy, liked to contrast what was true and authentic, that which is expressed in noble simplicity, with the false and theatrical, with whatever seeks outward effect but lacks moral substance. Pushkin, especially in the second phase of his literary career, loved to describe characters who are simple but heroic and full of a sense of their responsibility. He set them in contrast with dandies draped in affected 'Byronism,' the assumed 'Child Harold-ism' which was then the 'sickness of the age.' This same opposition

---

18 We are reminded of Tyutchev's famous poem about Christ walking on foot, in the guise of a serf, across the vast, barren plains of Russia.

19 And yet in Dostoevsky there is a nostalgia for simplicity too, an admiration for the spiritual authenticity found in people of humble spirit, whose character he sometimes sketches. See for example the little portraits 'The Centenarian' and 'Little Tableaux' in *The Diary of a Writer* for March 1876 and December 1873 respectively.

of the true and simple man who is not given to grand speeches, but reveals his worth at moments of crisis, over against the empty talker who is always living 'for show' and is unreliable and without spiritual consistency, this same opposition we find in Leo Tolstoy's writing, in his Caucasian story *The Foray*, for example, or in his *Sebastopol Sketches,* and above all in *War and Peace.*

Extolled as it was by all the great writers of Russia, this simplicity had its roots in the moral life inspired by religious experience.

In closing this chapter I would like to quote Yuri Samarin's well-known letter to Baroness Raden [20] on the soul of the Russian peasant—as he came to know it during his prolonged stay in the country in 1872, in the district of Samara. Each Sunday after the Liturgy he managed to enter into conversations with the peasants on religious subjects. At the request of the peasants he began to explain the meaning of the chants, and the whole service of the Church, and then to expound to them the fundamentals of the Christian faith. 'I need hardly tell you that in these discussions I learned more than I taught. What a mystery is the religious life of a people abandoned and ignorant, as ours is. One wonders where it comes from. . . . Our clergy do not teach it, they are busy officiating and administering the Sacraments.' Samarin was shocked by the unbelievable religious ignorance of the people; even the 'Our Father' was being said in such a way that it had lost all meaning. 'And yet in all these uncultured minds there is an altar built by some unknown hand, as there was in Athens, to an "Unknown God." The real presence of a providential Will in every event of life is a fact so incontrovertible that when death comes to these people, who have never heard the word of God explained, they open the door to Him as if to a well-known visitor long awaited. They offer their souls to God in the literal sense of the word.' [21]

Is it possible to make generalizations on the basis of this penetrating but perhaps too limited observation? However that may be, it sheds a very interesting light on the religious soul of the

---

[20] Lady companion of the Grand Duchess Helena Pavlovna who, under Alexander II, was one of the promoters of the emancipation of the serfs.
[21] *Correspondence of G. Samarin with Baroness Raden* (1861–76), published by D. Samarin, Moscow, 1894, pp. 192ff.; cf. Tolstoy's beautiful *Three Deaths.*

Russian peasant in the middle of the last century. Another current in this religious life of the people, more consciously imbued with the Christian message, may be found in the *Tales of a Pilgrim to his Spiritual Father* (see the next chapter). The narrator of these 'Tales' is akin to Dostoevsky's figure of the pilgrim in *A Raw Youth: Makar Ivanovich*.

CHAPTER FIVE

TYPES OF THE JUST AMONG THE RUSSIAN PEOPLE

LET us begin with the image of the Christian mother. In families which lived in the old style, where an intense participation in the intellectual life of the West in its noblest manifestations was combined with a deep rootedness in the life and spirituality of the Orthodox Church, in those patriarchal families (for example) among the cultivated nobility which had retained a sense of the soil—and there were many of them in the nineteenth century— in such families the mother was the shining centre of all spiritual, domestic and social life. She it was who played the primary role in the religious education of the children. There is a scene in *War and Peace* in which Princess Mary is sitting with her husband, Nicolas Rostov, as he looks at the diary in which she has made notes on the deportment of her young children. This scene is taken from real life.

'Nicolas looked deeply into the shining eyes that were fixed on him, and then went on turning the pages and reading. In this diary everything was recorded in the life of the children that seemed important to their mother, everything that revealed the children's character or that suggested general ideas or methods of education. They were, for the most part, little insignificant trifles, but they did not appear as such to the mother, nor to the father, who for the first time was reading this book devoted to the children. Under the date of December 5th there was written, "Mitya was not good at table. Papa said not to give him any dessert. He was not given any, and what a sad and hungry look he had as he watched the others eating! I think that to punish children by denying sweets to them only develops their greed. Speak to Nicolas about this."

'Nicolas closed the notebook and looked at his wife. The shining eyes were fixed on him in silent interrogation (Did he approve of the diary or not?) But there could be no doubt about Nicolas's approval, nor, for that matter, about his admiration. "It isn't necessary, perhaps, to write it in such a pedantic style, it isn't even necessary, perhaps, to write it at all," thought Nicolas, but this constant, untiring tension of the soul, with no other end but the moral welfare of the children, filled him with admiration. If Nicolas could have been fully conscious of what he was feeling, he would have understood that the main element in the firm, tender and proud love which he had for his wife was precisely this feeling of astonishment in the face of her moral life, in the face of this world of exalted spirituality, almost inaccessible as far as he was concerned, in which his wife lived constantly.'

The image of his own mother, a wonderful person full of kindness, highly cultivated intellectually, with a fine heart full of gentleness, remained alive in Tolstoy's mind all his life. Although he had scarcely known her (she died when he was only one and a half years old), he always venerated her deeply.

Alexis Khomyakov (1804-60), the great religious thinker and a fervent Christian, had this to say about his mother, who was a woman with a lucid mind and of uncommon piety and force of character: 'I know that if I can be useful in any way, it is to my mother that I am indebted, it is to my mother that I owe my spiritual outlook, and the unshakeable firmness of this outlook. . . . Happy is the man who has had such a mother and teacher in his youth! And what a lesson in humility this conviction involves.' [1] Avdotya Petrovna, the mother of the celebrated Kireevsky brothers, Ivan and Peter, was the living centre of a little world of intense literary and religious thought. The radiance of her heart extended over and beyond the immediate members of her own family, and made her house an unforgettable centre of hospitality and maternal kindness for all those who were drawn there, especially the young friends and acquaintances of her two sons. One of these young men, the well-known Russian jurist and historian Constantin Kavelin (1818-84), has celebrated 'the shining, noble and beautiful figure of Avdotya Petrovna, who showed so much kindness, so much interest and friendly, inexhaustible attention to these young people as they were growing

[1] Letter to Mme. Mukhanova, A. S. Khomyakov, *Works* (in Russian), 1900, Vol. VIII, p. 405.

up.' [2] This glow of charity and active friendliness on the part of a Christian mother, extending beyond the boundaries of her own family and making the family home a centre of light and goodness for all who were abandoned and afflicted, is connected in my mind with certain mothers I have known personally. The flame of charity, gentleness, an inborn tact, a lofty culture, especially the cultivation of the heart, all this has a captivating charm. But it is especially 'spiritual fervour' which has characterized the Christian mothers I have known. Their whole moral life was nourished by prayer, and especially intercession, not only for loved ones, but also for all troubled persons who crossed their path. Christ was the centre of their lives, and it was the presence of Christ which they radiated in their unbounded compassion. I am thinking especially of one of them, who used to teach her children to go without their favourite toys in order to give them to poor children, and instructed them particularly in compassion. She herself lived a life of active compassion. In the chaotic and terrible time of the Bolshevik Revolution, when there was famine everywhere, this woman, already advanced in years and in very hard circumstances herself, still shared with those who were dying of hunger the extremely limited supplies of her own family. She herself refused almost all food, although she was suffering from exhaustion, that she might give her share to those who were starving, whether they belonged to her family or not. Hers was an outpouring of love and pity, an 'elemental,' spontaneous outpouring, so to speak, not the deliberate application of some theory, but a living thing, something which had taken hold of her. She could not do otherwise; this was her life, a life of self-denial, compassion and charity, but without grand words; sober and balanced, full of sensitivity and a friendly, shining sense of humour, full of spontaneous simplicity coupled with a great wisdom and refinement of soul and mind and a high level of culture. And the centre of this life, her constant inspiration, was Christ. Her mind was directed toward Christ in constant intercession. She did the housework, even at a very advanced age, even when this was no longer necessary, as if she were unable not to work, and then, the work done, she would devote her time to prayer. She would sometimes take a book and sit down, but when

[2] K. D. Kavelin, *Complete Works* (in Russian), Vol. III, pp. 1121ff.

she was alone she would pray with all the force and energy of her soul, in untiring intercession. Turned toward Christ, she lived in His presence and implanted Him in the souls of others. And this was combined in her with a highly developed intellect. She loved the great English and German poets, the French historians (especially Amédée Thierry), the great Christian mystics of the West and East, the ascetical and mystical teachers of the Orthodox Church (particularly the writings of Bishop Theophan of Vysha); and above all she loved the Bible. She took a very lively interest in all the vital problems of our times, and in the religious life of the human soul down through the centuries, the soul's search for God, and also in justice and respect for the human person in the life of nations. Her life centre was everywhere and always Christ, in His limitless condescension. These words from the Gospel were always a part of her life: 'Inasmuch as you have done it to one of the least of my brothers, you have done it to me.'

Such Christian mothers are the treasure of every nation, of every people. How many treasures of the spiritual life are due to such Christian mothers in Russia! There is, for example, the mother of the famous Aksakov brothers, a woman full of vigour and a fine spirit, who left a deep mark on her children. I would like simply to quote a few words from a letter she wrote in 1844 to her son Ivan, who was away from home at the time, on the day of his coming of age. 'Well, my dear grown-up son, begin your mature life now with God's blessing. May prayer and faith in God always accompany you. Do not let yourself become proud; do not rely too much on yourself . . . for He exists. *He exists.* He is the One who rules over all. How I would like to pour into your soul this warming faith!' [3] I would like to end this brief memorial to Christian womanhood with the words of Leo Tolstoy, dedicated to the memory of the one who had acted as a mother for him and his orphaned brothers and sisters—his aunt Tatyana Alexandrovna Yergolskaya:

'The dominant note of her life was her marvellous kindness, extending to all, and knowing no limits. She never spoke an evil

---

[3] cf. the picture of the Aksakov family life in a brief description written by Ivan Aksakov and published in the collection of his letters, Moscow, 1882 Vol. I (in Russian).

word of any one. She lived in an era when the distance set between masters and servants was very pronounced; she was born into a way of life that was steeped in these ideas. And yet she never took advantage of the rights of a mistress, except in order to help her servants. She never used words in an effort to teach people how to love, she never made moralizing speeches. Her influence lay in setting the spiritual beauty of love before your eyes. She did not do this with words; instead, she kindled the flame of love by her entire existence. It was not just a few isolated actions, but one single life of love. She carried out the inner task of love and peace, drew others to herself, and brought a special charm into all her relationships. And this atmosphere of love for those present and absent, the living and the dead, even for animals, was filled with joy.'

The Christian mother was more often than the father the link between family and Church, and she frequently acted as an intermediary between the family and the spiritual influence of the great Russian startsy of the nineteenth century. We have, for example, a great number of remarkable letters written by the famous starets Bishop Theophan of Vysha (1815–94) to mothers of families. To one, living under the burden of many difficulties and anxieties, he wrote: 'The mercy of God be with you! All that comes from God apart from our own choice is always the best thing for us. It is not only as a matter of faith, in an abstract way, that this is true; we always see that this is the case when we begin to analyse the circumstances of our own lives. Thus your present situation, so full of anxieties, your own sickness and that of your son, and the difficulties to which you have alluded—all this is the most useful thing for you and yours. Only it is necessary to pray, and in praying to thank God. And for unhappy things you should thank Him even more—you must salute God's law, which punishes you and instructs' (November 15, 1872). To the same person he also gives instruction of a more general character: 'Judge no one, and you will have God as your defender. You should always regulate your affairs in such a way that external things do not hinder the things internal' (November 18, 1871). 'The Lord is everywhere, and everywhere the same. No place brings us closer to Him or puts us farther away from Him. If He comes to you where you are, and if you feel Him, then why do you wish to change your abode? You are looking for the Lord? Very well; but seek Him within yourself. He is not far from each of us. The Lord is very near to those who call on Him in all sincerity. Find a place in your heart, and enter there with the Lord. This is the Lord's reception room. Whoever meets the Lord, meets Him there. Nor has he designated any other place for this encounter' (April 17, 1872). 'May God bless you to persevere in the rule of interior life which you have chosen. The attention you give to all that it involves is the essential thing in a well ordered Christian life' (July 6, 1871).

To another mother he suggests how to prepare herself with her children, during Lent, for Confession and Holy Communion. To a father of a family who is a convert he recommends especially pity toward the needy: 'Especially, help those who are in need. If any one comes to you in tears, never let him leave without having dried his tears.'

•   •   •

I would like now to glance rapidly over several other types of righteousness which have played an important role in the religious history of the Russian people.

Suffering accepted for Christ's sake and in Christ's name plays a central part in all Christian experience. We have already seen how the first Russian saints represent this type of suffering—the young brothers Boris and Gleb. In general the type of a suffering just man, a kind of Christian Job, has flowered richly in Russia as also in other Christian lands. It can even be considered as representative of all popular Russian piety at its best. Ivan Turgenev found inspiration in the most profound and authentic sources of the religious life of the people when, in his little story 'Living Relics,' he sketched the touching figure of a young peasant woman, once healthy and robust. Seized by a sudden and mysterious illness, she watched her body wither and waste away; and now finds herself condemned to total immobility. She can only move one of her hands slightly. Her body has shrunk to the size of a little child's, her head alone remains beautiful and striking. Day and night during the summer she lies without movement in a shed, and in winter in the *predbanik,* the small heated ante-room of a peasant bath-house. She is full of infinite gratitude for the tiniest joys of life, for the least sign of attention on the part of men. She senses and recognizes the slightest breeze, the rays of the sun, she is filled with joy when she hears some bees, or sees the flight of a butterfly or a sparrow. She loves the coming and going of a lark which in the summer builds its nest in the shed. She bears no grudge as she submits herself to the will of God. And the narrator, who had known her when she was the young beauty of the village, is overwhelmed by this encounter.

Or there is the peasant Mikhail Bezrukov, of the district of Ufa, who died at the end of the nineteenth century. He too had been struck suddenly in the flower of his age by a paralysis, after exhausting himself in the field, and his body became covered with running sores. He suffered terribly, was unable to move, and at the moments of sharpest pain would murmur against God. Then a moral change took place: he accepted his suffering, and little by little he became the shining centre of an intense religious life. Inhabitants of the village and people from the most distant places came to ask his counsel, and to seek his prayers. The great pains gradually disappeared, but he remained paralysed; now full of patience and humility, a man of constant prayer.[4]

Asceticism is intimately bound up with the Christian life. Certain forms of radical asceticism still existed in Russia in the nineteenth century, in particular but characteristic instances recalling the life of St. Alexis, so popular in the West throughout the medieval period. These were cases of the renunciation of all the advantages of life, the renunciation of high social rank, family, fortune; but without entrance into the monastic life, for this was the rejection of all forms of life accepted and venerated by the world. There were then cases of total renunciation, where the holder of an honoured position would descend to the bottom of the social scale (so clearly stratified in Russia) and mix with simple people, with the poor among the non-privileged classes, and would become one with them, even poorer than they, having no home, no means, no family, no position however modest. Such people might become simple pilgrims without a place to sleep, or poor labourers who would divide their life between work and prayer. We find an example of this renunciation of the glitter of the

[4] For a detailed account of his life see Poselyanin, *Raiskie tsvety russkoy zemli* (in Russian), 1909.

world, a much more radical one than that which takes place in modern monasticism, in the mysterious existence of Fedor Kuzmich, who died in Tomsk, Siberia, in 1864, past the age of eighty. He had obviously been an important person, a man of culture familiar with the life of politics, diplomacy and war in his time, about the beginning of the nineteenth century; a man who knew foreign languages, with a fine bearing, a majestic gait, an innate distinction. Was this Alexander I, who had perhaps left his throne in a clandestine manner and simulated his death with the help of close friends in the remote little town of Taganrog, making his death 'official' in 1825 by passing off the body of a dead soldier as his own? No one can be certain even now, and many facts if weighed seriously speak for the probability if not the certainty of this story, which at first seems so fantastic and incredible.[5] In any case this Fedor Kuzmich was a true Christian who in his life of self-denial and humility became a centre of the spiritual life. In a charming little book which describes some of the most profound and intimate aspects of Russian religious life—*The Letters of a Pilgrim to his Spiritual Father* (dating probably from the 40s or 50s of the last century)—we have the figure of another great nobleman who, as an act of contrition and in an effort to quiet his bruised and troubled conscience, had left all to become a penniless pilgrim.

The pilgrims, the 'idiots,' the 'fools for Christ' (*urodivi Khrista radi*) and the collectors of alms who would travel on foot all over Russia gathering large sums of money for the construction of churches, promoting the construction of new churches in all parts of the land . . . and other such figures . . . how typical they are of the currents of religious experience in the vast ocean of the people's life! And how many false pilgrims, false ascetics, false men of God there were among them, living on the credulity of the people! But falsehood goes hand in hand with the truth, like a shadow. Many of these wanderers lived an authentic and often deep-rooted religious life. I turn here to the *Tales of a Pilgrim* because it is a text which is now translated and readily accessible.[6]

[5] See, among others, the excellent little monograph by Krupensky, *The Mystery of the Emperor* (in Russian), Paris, published some years before the Second World War.

[6] First published in Russian in 1881; see the French translation by Jean Gauvain, *Récits d'un pèlerin à son père spirituel,* Cahiers du Rhône, Neuchâtel, 1943 and the English translation *Tales of a Pilgrim,* London, S.P.C.K.

It is a remarkable work. The author of this work is a special kind of pilgrim, a simple young peasant who reads the *Philocalia,* the celebrated collection of ascetical and mystical writings, and devotes his time to continual prayer. One winter he spends in an abandoned forest hut, dug out of the ground (*zemlyanka*), far from all human habitations, practising continual prayer and reading in his precious book. And here are his unexpected encounters with persons coming from the most varied walks of life, yet all united in the practice of interior prayer and their love of the *Philocalia.* It is a sort of silent and spontaneous 'confraternity' of adherents of the mystical life which is introduced to us in the pages of this little book. Here, for example, is an officer escorting prisoners to Siberia—a man of piety who always carries his New Testament with him under his uniform, a man of compassion having the fear of God, in spite of his work. Or again, here is a hospitable and pious couple—husband and wife—who receive pilgrims in their house and bear witness to a radiant and active Christian goodness. On the other hand the pilgrim describes for us his own interior life and the transfiguration of all creation in the beams of the Divine Word—a transfiguration which he feels at moments of inner exaltation. 'Sometimes,' he says, 'I would feel a burning love for Jesus Christ and for all of God's creation. At times sweet tears of recognition of the Lord would flow of their own accord, at times a comforting warmth coming from the heart would penetrate my whole being, and I would feel the presence of God all round me.' 'Not only in the inner recesses of my soul,' he says farther on, 'did I feel this, but every external thing would also appear in a glorious aspect and would continually invite me to love and sing the praise of God. Men, trees, plants, animals, all seemed so close to me, everywhere I recognized the mark of Christ.' All creatures testify to 'the love of God for men, everything is filled with an impulse toward God and sings His glory. And by this I understood what the *Philocalia* calls "the knowledge of the hidden meaning of creation," and I have seen in what manner one can deal with God's creation.' [7]

The authenticity of this little book is corroborated indirectly

[7] *Otkrovennye raskazy stranika,* 1881, pp. 39–40, 93.

by a similar figure described by Dostoevsky in his novel *A Raw Youth,* another pilgrim, but already in his old age—the moving figure of old Makar Ivanovich. As with the author of the *Tales,* the world becomes transfigured in the eyes of Makar Ivanovich by his feeling of the presence of God, a Presence which is the great 'mystery' of creation. 'What is this mystery? Everything is a mystery, my friend, in everything there is the mystery of God. Whether it is a little bird singing, or the stars shining like a huge choir in the night sky—it is always the same mystery. . . . If I feel better, I'll go on a pilgrimage again in the spring. Everything is in thee, O Lord, and I am in thee—accept me!'

A great deal has been written about the 'fools for Christ's sake,' some of it true and some of it false. At times this was simply a desire to shock people, sometimes even a pious mask for cynicism or laziness, or again it could be a genuine mental defect, a congenital 'idiocy.' Sometimes such idiocy was combined—strange as it may seem—with real depths of the spiritual life which concealed but did not put an end to the defects of intellect. This last condition was frequent enough, and those who were 'poor in spirit' in the literal sense of the word could be true servants of God. Sometimes, finally, there were great ascetics and servants of God, perfectly normal from the psychological viewpoint, who would hide an extraordinarily rich religious life under the eccentricities of a feigned madness for the sake of humility, that they might be despised and scorned by men. These latter were the only ones who really corresponded to the designation 'fools for Christ's sake.' A great number of these fools for the love of Christ (especially from the fourteenth to the seventeenth century) have been venerated by the Russian people; about thirty have been canonized. If one looks into the twelve volumes of the *Lives of Righteous Persons in Russia in the eighteenth and nineteenth centuries* the number of *urodivye* is comparatively large. For example, the one volume for the month of September presents, out of a total of thirty-four, five biographies of *urodivye.* Classic Russian literature sometimes gives us illustrations of this type. It may be a pseudo-saint, as described by Dostoevsky in the comic scene in *Demons.* Or there is the moving figure of the poor fool Grisha in Leo Tolstoy's *Childhood* (1853). In his secret prayer this poor fool pours out before God the hidden riches of his ardent, innocent soul. . . . 'I pushed my head gradually through the half open door,' Tolstoy writes, 'and was afraid to breathe. Grisha remained motionless on his knees; his chest heaving with deep sighs; in the dark pupil of his eye there was a tear gleaming in the moonlight.'

' "Thy will be done!" he cried out suddenly with an indescribable expression, and touched his forehead against the ground sobbing like a child. . . . .O Grisha, what a Christian! Your faith was so great that you felt the presence of God!' (Chapter XII).

Through the centuries of Russian history the authentic 'fools for Christ' have often spoken their word of truth in a startling and courageous manner (especially in the fifteenth and sixteenth centuries) to the great ones of this world, before whom all others quailed.

．　　．　　．

In general the social function of a holy life or the *social mission* of righteous people and saints is a theme of very great importance for Russia, as it is also for other countries. It is not true that Russian piety has lacked a philanthropic and social impulse, that it has remained purely contemplative, ignoring the life and sufferings of men. Russian monasticism, besides its contemplative element, manifests also an eminently social concern : a tremendous outburst of charity in the service of one's neighbour. The great saints were full of compassion. The monastic tradition of the Christian East, when it penetrated into Russia, even accentuated this element of service to one's neighbour so inseparable from the Christian life. For the people were ignorant, poor and forsaken, and there was a great need for someone to be concerned about them and about their spiritual welfare. The same cause injected a strong and active philanthropic quality into the great monastic institutions of the medieval period in the West.

The common people stood in great need of help. Many examples could be cited of the philanthropic activity of the large monastic centres in medieval Russia. Professor Smirnov, the eminent historian of Russian Christianity, has gathered together many pieces of information which are characteristic of this trend, in his excellent little book *How the Saints and Ascetics of Old Russia ministered to their Neighbours.*[8] This corresponds exactly to that element of compassion and active piety, a piety that would go beyond the boundaries of a moral 'bourgeoisie,' that pity which we have stressed as a major element in the religious and moral life of the Russian people. How remarkable, for example, are these words from the Testament of St. Paphnutius of Borovsk (d. 1477): 'Do not buy for me a coffin of oak wood; instead of the coffin use the money to buy some white loaves (*kalachi*) and distribute them to the poor. As for me, wrap me in the bark of a tree, dig a hole in the ground, and put me in.'[9] St. Joseph of Volokolamsk, the disciple of Paphnutius, was especially full of this active charity. During a great famine a huge crowd gathered one day, from all directions . . . 7,000 persons not including children . . . in front of the monastery gates. St. Joseph gave orders that all should be fed; as for the little starving children, he sheltered and cared for them for a long time in a special hostel in the monastery. When, after some time, the holy abbot had the parents summoned to come and take their children back again, no one came, and it was necessary to build a special home for these children, and to care for them. 'In his pity the holy man nourished these children whom he had not brought into the world, and took care of them as if they were his own.'[10] Another great representative of the monastic life, St. Cornelius of Komel (d. 1537) was also a man of outstanding charity. St. Daniel of Pereyaslav (d. 1540) transformed his monastery into a shelter for invalids and a hospital for the sick people brought to him from all over the country. 'He received them with great joy in the monastery, nourished them and took care of them.'[11] There are a great many such examples, and this is, after all, only natural. A true Christian would not be able to live without compassion for his neighbour.

. . .

Let us add a few words here about *confessors of truth*, those who have spoken the truth to the powerful and great men of this world. The Russian Church has not always been passive and

[8] S. I. Smirnov, *Kak sluzhili miru podvishniki drevney Russi*, Sergiev Lavra, 1903.
[9] Quoted by Smirnov, p. 52.
[10] According to the ancient *Life*, quoted by Smirnov, p. 55.
[11] Old biographical manuscript, quoted by Smirnov, p. 62.

silent in the face of injustice. Her misfortune was that she often depended too much on the State, especially since the eighteenth century but also in the sixteenth and seventeenth centuries; so much so that a great number of her representatives lost not only their independence at the hands of the State but also, sometimes, even their spiritual freedom. A spirit of obsequiousness and careerism swayed the hearts of a great many prelates. The danger that exists to-day is on a much larger scale. The chief difference is that in the time of the Tsars the temporal power was always, in principle if not in fact, intimately connected to the Church by the bonds of faith. The power in modern Russia, on the other hand, is atheistic and hostile to faith in God, and is absolutely ruthless and cynical in its moral outlook. And yet in spite of this great difference, which cannot be exaggerated, there is a certain similarity between the dangers the Church faced then and the dangers she faces to-day. For this reason, as we end this chapter, we must say something about the courageous defenders and confessors of the truth.

As early as the eleventh century St. Theodosius of the Pechersky monastery near Kiev spoke the truth with courage to the great ones of this world. He wrote a severe letter criticizing Prince Svyatoslav, who had seized the throne from his elder brother by driving him out of Kiev, and compared Svyatoslav with the murderer Cain. St. Gregory the Wonder-Worker, from the same monastery, was thrown into the Dnieper by Prince Rostislav, whose crimes he had denounced. St. John, abbot of the Pechersky monastery, condemned Prince Svyatopolk II for his rapacity and oppression of the common people. In 1430, in the Vologda region in northern Russia, the abbot St. Gregory denounced the savage Prince Dimitry Shenyaka to his face for the crimes and endless cruelties of the civil war he had unleashed. 'Prince Dimitry,' he said, 'have you not read in Holy Scripture that judgment without mercy awaits him who has shown no mercy? You, even you, have committed acts that are opposed to Christian faith . . .' The great St. Philip, Metropolitan of Moscow in the sixteenth century, was not afraid, as a good and faithful pastor of his flock, to try to influence the violent and furious nature of the criminal Ivan the Terrible to preach justice and mercy to him, and to denounce his crimes and impious acts. He paid for this with his life.

113

H

We also find confessors and martyrs for the faith in Russia in more recent times. We must pause here, however, since we have now come to a turning point in Russian religious history. For the first time the *martyr* appears among the countless representatives of the Church in Russia. This martyrdom equals or perhaps surpasses (in point of numbers) the great persecutions of the first centuries of Christianity. A large number of bishops, thousands of priests and a countless number of faithful have suffered for their loyalty to Christ and the Church. Very often the demand has been made by civil authority: Deny the faith, and you will be set free. I quote from reliable witnesses. These show clearly enough that it was *the faith which was being persecuted.* Where are we to begin in describing these afflictions? Here is a long procession of priests and bishops being deported (among them old men who could scarcely walk); dressed almost in rags, most of them without winter clothing. They are leaving the city of Archangel with a crowd of people accompanying them, seized with pity, and weeping openly (trying not to be noticed, some women are hastily giving them their coats, woollen scarves, knitted sweaters, and jackets). The procession sets out, in the dead of winter, across the blank stretches of snow, toward the banks of the Pechora river, over 400 miles east of Archangel. Two-thirds of the deportees die on the way, killed by the cold on the arctic plain; some of them are left to die slowly alone. Here are the priests beaten with steel bars in one of the Soviet concentration camps (invented in Russia long before the terrible camps in Germany), as we learn from the report of one who managed to escape with a Finnish passport.[12] Here is the slow and dreadful martyrdom of Anthony, the venerable archbishop of Archangel, an old man with a good and simple heart, who used to share all he had with the poor. His pastoral cross was torn from his neck. There could be no formal charge laid against him, since he was not involved in affairs of State or any intrigue. He was a cheerful pastor, with a good and simple nature, a true bishop, and that was enough. He lay on the ground, without fresh air and without water, all through the days of summer, in suffocating heat, in a small over-crowded cell, in the filthiest conditions, begging for water. They gave him nothing

[12] Kichin, *Prisoners of the Guépéou,* New York, 1930.

but beatings. Persons who were devoted to him and others imprisoned with him have preserved accurate details of his imprisonment and death. Here too are the Metropolitans Arseny of Novgorod, Cyril of Kazan, Ilarion and Peter of Krutitsa, the Archimandrite Taube, and a great many other bishops of the Church who have remained steadfast in prison and true to their faith, to the point of death.

Here again is the trial and execution of Metropolitan Benjamin of Petrograd. A spirit of early Christian martyrdom inspired everything he did during his 'trial,' if a tissue of obviously false testimony—often refuted by the defence—can be called a trial. But the verdict had been determined in advance. The defence lawyer Gurevich (not a Christian, incidentally, but a Jew) was a man of energy, intelligence and noble character, who had the courage to defend the metropolitan in a lost cause. As he said in a lecture in France, he was deeply moved by the spiritual atmosphere which radiated from the Metropolitan and his fellow prisoners. This was the spirit of primitive Christian heroism, a fervent faith which won hearts. But Mr. Gurevich's account goes further. Certainly he admired the simple, gentle heroism of the Metropolitan and the other prisoners, their greatness of soul, but it was not this which struck and overwhelmed him during the course of the trial. 'It was,' he said, 'that behind and above the Metropolitan and the other accused prisoners something greater could be felt, *a living reality,* to which they were only bearing witness. What more can be said when one is speaking of martyrs? These were not just heroes, they were witnesses to the truth.' Here are a few words from Metropolitan Benjamin's last letter, written on the eve of his death: 'We must now go beyond our science and self-sufficiency, leaving the field open for grace.'

We are reminded here of the words of the Epistle to the Hebrews (11: 32). 'What shall I say then? For there is not time to speak' of all the heroes of the faith. The limitations of my task compel me to bring this short sketch to an end. But again, think of those bishops imprisoned with common criminals who con-

---

[13] Described by a witness in Andrey Russinov's fine book *Die Grosse Tauschung,* Leipzig, 1939.

verted thieves and murderers to faith in God.[13] And there are too the 'wandering priests,' who go on foot and secretly from village to village, preaching in the name of God and administering the Sacraments. And the secret Easter Liturgies in the forests of the Vologda region.[14] And the feats of heroism and Christian courage which have been demonstrated very widely among the people, among simple people, among the humble village women (for example) who have held up their heads before examining magistrates and preferred detention and torture to apostasy. A special chapter in this Christian epic is the exile of bishops to the arctic lands of Siberia, sometimes well beyond the Arctic Circle, in little huts covered with snow, in a climate where it is difficult even to survive, with 65 degrees of frost in the winter, the arctic night lasting almost half the year, and in summer the hordes of mosquitoes everywhere. It was under such conditions that the *locum tenens* of the Russian patriarch, Metropolitan Peter of Krutitsa and the Metropolitan Cyril of Kazan were exiled, and died. We have some remarkable letters written by the young Bishop Damascene of Glukhov to his people while he was in exile beyond the Arctic Circle. As he celebrated the Holy Eucharist in his little hut, surrounded by mountains of snow, he would see 'all those so near and dear to me standing with me before the altar.' 'I believe,' he wrote in another place, 'that in these dark days the right thing is for the faithful to let their personal sufferings dissolve in the common suffering, and that they strengthen themselves by recalling the warning given in the Word of God concerning the inevitability of the trials and sufferings which must come upon the world.' And here is the voice of Metropolitan Cyril of Kazan resounding across the arctic night: 'Let the Holy Spirit who dwells forever in the Church lead us through the furnace of the present trials to the great revelation of His Glory!'

Or consider Bishop Platon, confined in a cave at Dorpat with some Protestant pastors and professors of theology, and waiting with them to be shot by the Bolsheviks, keeping his courage and peace of soul, in the suffocating atmosphere of the little cave where so many people were crowded together. He comforted the others;

---

[14] cf. Schwarz, *In Wologda's weissen Waldern*, Hans Harder-Verlg, 1938.

and with them prepared himself in all humility and serenity to accept death for the Lord's sake.[15]

During the war the wave of persecutions which had broken over the Church was calmed. But the dangers were not over. After the truce or period of outward calm, which was filled, as we have seen, with other hazards, in the realm of morals, a new wave of religious persecutions has spread over Soviet Russia, especially since 1960. But the courage and faith of the martyrs has not been in vain, they have fertilized and strengthened the Church. They have demonstrated *the living power of Christ* before the entire world. It is a great work of universal significance which has been accomplished in the Russian Church over these years of persecution.

[15] He himself and some of the Protestant pastors were shot, among them the theology professor T. Hahn. The others escaped death. Their execution had been postponed, and in the meantime anti-Bolshevik troops entered the city, and set them free. We are indebted to them for the account of Bishop Platon's heroic end.

CHAPTER SIX

THE INTERIOR WORLD OF RUSSIAN
SAINTS AND STARTSY [1]

LET us turn our attention to the inner life of the Spirit.
The 'silence of the heart,' a great peace—this is the impression
that one gets on being introduced to the world of the saints and
the great just men of Russia. Simplicity and calm, purity of
heart and restraint, inner balance and, on the other hand, constant
spiritual tension, sober and courageous virility, and finally gentleness and profound humility. . . . And then prayer, fervent, untiring prayer, as the point of departure and source of nourishment,
as the support and framework of this life-prayer in the direct-
ness of the heart, the constant interior turning to Jesus Christ
the Son of God, who has pity on sinners. All this new life has a
Christocentric orientation, is rooted in the invocation of our Lord
Jesus Christ. These, then, are the fundamental characteristics of
the piety of saints and just persons in Russia. This purity and
simplicity have about them a special perfume, the perfume of
authenticity. This is no hysterical effusion; there is a soberness here,
the mark of truth, of peace restored, of divine inspiration. Along
with this (we must repeat) there is a rigour towards the self,
an activeness, an unceasing spiritual combat, after the pattern of
the ascetical and mystical tradition of the greatest Fathers of the
East.

Let us try first to bring out the essential elements of the teaching
given by the masters of the spiritual life. The already quoted
Bishop Theophan of Vysha (1815–94) writes in a letter of direction: 'You should conquer your self-love (*samougodie*), as the
Saviour has commanded: If any one would follow me, let him
deny himself. . . . When you have done that you will no longer
need to ask how you ought to live to attain salvation. . . . You will
see clearly that there is no other way to obtain salvation than that

---

[1] See my article in the review *Dieu vivant*, Paris, 1946, No. 6.

118

of renouncing self. This is indeed the narrow way that leads to life.' [2]

It is the renunciation of or contempt for self, then, that is the dominant note. Here is where the new life springs forth. The new life is, in fact, just that. It must be won through constant interior struggle. Without combat there is no new reality. It is a virile ideal that is preached here: the figures of the just and the saints have the stamp of virility.

I would like to shed some light on this interior reality by quoting further from the correspondence of Bishop Theophan:

'The Lord is the Commander-in-Chief. You are the warrior. He expects you to repulse the enemy. Do not let Him down.' [3]

'. . . seek and you will find. And yet there will be struggle. Without combat the warrior is but a poor soldier. Everything is learned in combat.' [4]

'The Christian life runs into many obstacles at the very start, and further on there are more. Whoever enters upon this life, let him arm himself with a firm courage, that he may approach without fear the struggles and obstacles which await him.' [5]

'Force yourself to acquire the habit of standing watch over your heart, and do not give free rein to your thoughts, feelings or instincts, if they are not moved by a spirit that is pleasing to God, but suppress them at once.' [6]

'There is a way to spiritually raise up the Cross in your heart. You do this when you make the firm resolution to crucify yourself or mortify your passions, something which is so essential for Christians that according to the Apostle only those belong to Christ who have crucified their flesh with its passions and desires.' [7]

'This spiritual combat should never be relaxed; it must be taken up again and again. If you have fallen, do not despair, get up at once with the firm resolve to fall no more. And continue your struggle.' It is especially important not to be discouraged, not to give up the fight. There is, on the other hand, the no less categori-

[2] *Sobranie pisem Svatitelya Feofana* (The Correspondence of Bishop Theophan), Vol. III, Moscow, 1898, p. 4.
[3] ibid., Vol. IV, p. 96.
[4] ibid., p. 109.
[5] ibid., Vol. III, pp. 164–5.
[6] ibid., p. 215.
[7] ibid., p. 165.

cal affirmation: *We can win nothing without His help*. In Him—in the Lord Jesus Christ alone—is the power, the help, the succour. Without Him we can do nothing.

The two points are not mutually exclusive: the demand for an intense spiritual activity, for a constant and courageous struggle . . . and the fundamental conviction that salvation lies *only in Him*, in the Lord Jesus Christ, and that without Him we are able to do nothing at all. They are, rather, mutually conditioned. The two dispositions grow together into a *living synthesis* of the Life in Christ.

For this activity, this virile combat is by its essence a turning to God, a constant stretching forth toward Him, an appeal and a prayer. The whole of the interior life is centred in prayer.

'Whoever takes up the spiritual life can never say: I will do this, I will do that. Force yourself to seek God without ceasing, like a fish caught in the ice striking out round itself with its tail. And you will receive what it pleases the Lord to give you, and *when* it pleases Him.

'One must seek Him and cry to Him out of a contrite heart: Save me, according to Thine own will. . . . For there is salvation only in Him. But let this abandonment of self to God include a firm zeal, full of self-denial, that His holy will may be done.' [8]

'Whoever does not labour spiritually with all his powers and makes no effort to feel his own impotence, and does not utter the cry for help which arises out of this impotence, will not obtain this awareness. . . . You must do this: in the sense of your own impotence call on Him for help; and even after having accomplished something, continue in the awareness of your own powerlessness.' [9]

'Seek and you will find. This is the immutable law of all success on the path of spiritual progress. Nothing comes without difficulty. The help of God is always ready and close at hand, but it is given only to those who seek and give themselves up to hardship, and only when those who seek have exhausted all their own resources and given themselves up to prayer with all their heart: O Lord, come to my rescue. But if the least confidence in one's own

[8] ibid., Vol. V, pp. 22–3 and 28–9.
[9] ibid., Vol. VI, p. 52.

resources still remains, the Lord will not intervene, as if He were saying. "Are you hoping to attain your goal on your own? Very well then, hope a little longer . . ." And no matter how long you hope, nothing will come of it. May the Lord give you a contrite spirit, a contrite and humble heart!' [10]

'The Lord is able, knows how to, and wishes to save us. He looks for those He will be able to save. And He saves all who come to Him. Those who wish to save themselves are the only ones who fall short of salvation.' [11]

'We have the Lord, the one Lord, the only Saviour, without whom we are unable to do anything good at all. He is always near. Turn then to Him.' [12]

'You must not rely upon your own powers. On the contrary, whenever any trouble overwhelms your heart, you should turn at once to the Lord, and not cease calling on Him until your anxiety is calmed.' [13]

'You must have the feeling of a man who is drowning in the sea and has caught hold of a board that can hold him up and carry him over the deep. He constantly feels that he is about to go under, but at the same time he is touching the board of salvation. This is an exact picture of every soul proceeding in the Lord along the path of salvation. It feels that it is sinking, yet at the same time there is salvation in the Lord.' [14]

In short: 'Embrace suffering. God will give you the strength. The awareness of your own weakness is the first step in obtaining the help of God.' [15]

'For we must not cease thinking and feeling that success in the spiritual life, in all its external manifestations, is a friut of God's grace. This new spiritual life proceeds entirely from the thrice holy Spirit of God. We have our own spirit, it is true, but it is impotent. It acquires strength only when the grace of God covers it with its shadow.' [16]

One's entire life should be lived in a stream of prayer: 'The

[10] ibid., Vol. IV, p. 41.
[11] ibid., Vol. V, p. 47.
[12] ibid., p. 49.
[13] ibid., p. 109.
[14] ibid., pp. 25–6.
[15] ibid., pp. 89–90.
[16] ibid., p. 163.

Lord is near. If you turn to Him with anguished supplications and cries of distress, you will be heard at once.' [17]

'With fervour make all your spiritual needs known to the Lord, and He will help you. Prayer is the breath of the spiritual life, as you know very well already. It is useless, therefore, to waste words on this subject. Pray more fervently, pray without ceasing—the Lord is near, and His relief is near at every moment.' [18]

We must become used to living constantly in the presence of the Lord, used to spending our life in ceaseless contemplation, and used to walking before Him.

'The most important thing is to walk before God, or in God's sight, with the feeling that God has His eyes upon you, that He is looking into your heart and soul, and sees everything . . . this feeling is the strongest lever for advancing the interior life.' [19]

'When you withdraw into yourself, it is necessary to place yourself in the presence of the Lord, and to live in this way without turning your spiritual eyesight away from Him. This is the interior hermitage; live there alone before God.' [20]

That is the central meaning of the Holy Communion : 'You have received the Lord. Only let Him fill your soul to overflowing. The Lord is near. If you speak to Him, no spiritual distress will come upon you that you will not be able to conquer and subdue.' [21]

From this a completely new attitude is born, extending not only into the spiritual but also into the physical life.

'Keep the muscles of the body taut and disciplined. Give no freedom whatever to the sybarite of the body.' 'Your body must be subjected to the rigorous discipline of the soldier.' [22]

'We are called not to kill our bodies, but to mortify them, not provide for them in ways that would gratify their lusts (Rom. 13 : 14). The rule to observe is to discipline the body in a reasonable way, without indulgence and complacency.' [23]

·This spirit of discipline, fear of God, and of a life in the presence of the Lord, engenders an inner maturity, gravity, modera-

[17] ibid., Vol. III, p. 207.
[18] ibid., Vol. IV, p. 104.
[19] ibid., p. 75; cf. Vol. III, p. 220; Vol. IV, pp. 40ff.
[20] ibid., Vol. IV, p. 40.
[21] ibid., p. 88; cf. Vol. IV, p. 85.
[22] ibid., Vol. IV, pp. 96, 105.
[23] ibid., p. 165.

tion and spiritual soberness which flee and scorn all excesses of feeling.

'The most important fruit of prayer is not warmth or inner sweetness, but fear of God and contrition. This feeling must constantly be stirred up, one must always live and breathe in it.' 'Spiritual activity is not made up of ecstasies. Its best manifestation is a contrite spirit, a humble and contrite heart. Since you have written that you feel better when you place yourself in God's presence, do this always.' [24]

There is a virile and quiet attitude of mind here which has its ultimate crown in humility.

The *startsy* abhorred all spiritual aberrations, all excessive emotionalism, looking on such things with deep mistrust. This is illustrated in the correspondence of the celebrated *starets* Makar of Optino.

A young woman had decided to enter a convent. She received her mother's consent, and wished to live in extreme poverty from that moment on. She begged her mother to furnish the cell being built for her in the convent as poorly as possible. The *starets* Makar warns her against impetuous zeal, which conceals much pride and complacency:

'You are asking your mother to furnish everything for you in the simplest way possible. But according to the Holy Fathers we ought not to kill our bodies but our passions. I warn you again of this danger: do not take it into your head to become holy all of a sudden. Be careful. You have asked questions about prayer. When we pray we ought to have great humility, and this serves to break down our wilfulness and the exaggerated opinion we have of ourselves. Take care not to wish to pray only in spirit, you are not yet capable of this. You will fall at once into illusion. Pray simply. He who bestows the gift of prayer to the one who prays will also give you this pure prayer, in the spirit, but only if you become truly humble and consider your sin. In this way the soul becomes contrite and the heart is humbled . . .'

'You are reading the works of *starets* Athanasius. You are undertaking things which are not suitable for you. You have no idea how necessary it is to humble your thoughts. Let us say that

[24] ibid., pp. 176, 191.

you accomplish everything that is written in this book. You would not then be able to escape pride and self-sufficiency, those enemies which insinuate themselves into your nature so quietly that you don't notice them. It will do you great harm. But with humility you also gain peace. If in all you have done you have reaped no spiritual profit, but only interior trouble, it is clear that you do not have humility. You are thinking only of external things and are not thinking about uprooting your passions. This is why it is necessary for you to be able to take counsel with someone who is right there with you, and to repress your wilfulness and pride . . .'

'You continue to aspire to the most elevated experiences of the spiritual life and to rules which are not yet suitable for you. You ought rather to follow simply the humble path, as others do without experiencing inner turmoil. You must no longer yield to interior anxiety when you have committed some blunder or mistake, but go down into the depth of humility, and rise again in penitence—and soon you will discover the right path . . .' (Nov. 4, 1858).

'You ask me what is the ultimate goal of prayer and you quote the words of John Climacus, saying that prayer by night consecrates the works of the day. But does this really fit your present spiritual situation? To whom were these words addressed? Ask the Reverend Mother M. to instruct you on this point, and all the others. She sees your spiritual state and will tell you what is useful. If not, you will get up at night to pray, and in so doing will condemn the others who do not, and will set yourself above them. You desire to enter into what is truly "spiritual activity," but this consists in rejecting your own will and your own judgment.' [25]

This *simplicity* and *absence of pretension* are characteristic. The great master of the ascetical and mystical life, St. Nil Sorsky (1453–1508), wrote long before: 'We should not begin too quickly with what is too high for us. . . The best thing is to stay midway between . . .' For the goal of all this is to grow in *humility*.

I would like to conclude these words about the life in God by referring to a remarkable letter, addressed by the celebrated

[25] cf. *Twenty-three Letters from Starets Makar of Optino to Mme. S.I.N.* (in Russian), Moscow, 1908.

starets Paisy Velichkovsky (1722–94) of Moldavia to M. P. Protasseva, his spiritual daughter, the Superior of a small community of nuns in the province of Nizhni Novgorod. The letter is a rich synthesis of spiritual counsel. What stands out particularly here is the great kindness and condescension toward one's neighbour, the boundless charity, the mortification of the old man and, as the fundamental attitude, humility. Thus the *starets* describes the duties of the Superior toward the sisters entrusted to her care: 'Teach them the way of salvation by giving them—with God's help—an example of good works, by the careful observation of the commandments of the Gospel, by love for God and your neighbour, by kindness and humility, by the deep peace of Christ expressed in your dealings with others, by a truly maternal pity, by patience and long-suffering, by prayers accompanied by tears, consoling them and encouraging them to do better. Support all their burdens and frailties with God's love, be on fire with God's love for them, teach them diligently to obey God in all things, to restrain or rather to mortify their own will. As for yourself, you ought always in the secrecy of your heart and soul regard yourself as dust before God, as the greatest sinner among men.' [26]

. . .

Let us pass on now to the actual lives of these saints.

We shall have much to say, of course, about their humility, since this is the dominant element in their lives. Their entire life is one of humility. Theodosius of Pechersk (eleventh century) and Sergius of Radonezh (fourteenth century) were noted for their exceptional humility. They wore the most shabby clothes, they did not refuse to do the most menial tasks (even when Sergius was an abbot). They shunned all honours and distinctions (even when they were the noted counsellors and spiritual directors of reigning princes). '*A humble gentleness*—such was the fibre of the personality of St. Sergius of Radonezh,' wrote Professor Fedotov, and with good reason.[27] We know the story of the peasant who was unwilling to believe that the man with the poor, patched garments,

[26] Quoted from unpublished letters of Paisy by Archpr. S. Chetverikov in his work on *Paisy Velichkovsky*, Réval, 1938, Part II, pp. 49–50.

[27] G. P. Fedotov, *The Saints of Old Russia* (in Russian), Paris, YMCA Press, 1931, p. 143. On Russian saints see also the late Fr. Ivan Kologrivov's fine book *Essai sur la sainteté russe*, Editions Beyaert, Brussels, 1953.

digging so vigorously there, could be the celebrated abbot of the great monastery, and proceeded to insult him. Sergius, on his part, welcomed the peasant kindly and graciously, and invited him to the table of the monastery, making him sit at his side in the place of honour.[28] This humility, as we have said, goes hand in hand with a gentle kindness toward others. It can become a charitable ministry filling the whole of life. This was so among the *startsy* at Optino, and in other places, who put their whole life at the service of those who were suffering, those who had a real need for consolation and encouragement.

I would like to introduce here some excerpts from the life of St. Tikhon of Zadonsk (1724–83), written by his servant Chebotarev. A marvellous simplicity, candour and kindness radiate from this document. In him the life in God is united with a limitless charity toward one's neighbour.

The greater part of Chebotarev's writings deal with the time when Tikhon was living in the monastery of Zadonsk, after he had officially resigned the episcopal see of Voronezh (he had been Bishop of Voronezh from 1763–67) because of ill health (or, perhaps, guided by some inner voice). And yet the height of his work of spiritual counselling and service to the poor and afflicted came in this period. Thousands of people of all kinds streamed to him from near and far to relieve their material or spiritual needs, seeking from him some lesson or word of advice. He drew the nourishment for his inner life from prayer. Prayer was, so to speak, the axis of his inner being.

'It was his custom to spend the night without sleeping, and to lie down on his bed only at dawn,' writes his servant . . . 'unworthy as I am, I have witnessed this. During the night he would give himself to prayer, making deep prostrations. His prayer was ardent and never cold. It came from a contrite heart, so that at times he cried aloud, "Lord, have mercy on me! Lord, have pity on me!" and he would add, "O loving Father, have mercy!"[29] as he touched

---

[28] cf. the humility of the great hermit and founder of monasteries in northern Russia, St. Dimitry Prilutsky (d. 1392); see Konoplev, *The Saints of the Vologda Country* (in Russian), 1895, p. 37; cf. also 'Psikhologia nashikh pravednikov' (The Psychology of our Righteous Persons) in the review *Voprosy filosofii i psikhologii*, Moscow, 1906, Vol. 84, pp. 334–5.

[29] *'Kormilets, pomilui!'*

his head on the ground. All this was inspired in him by a great inner flame and by his love of God. Then, about midnight, he would go into the outer room and softly, in a voice full of feeling, chant the holy psalms. When he was in a sad mood, he would chant "It is good that thou hast afflicted me . . ." etc., and other consoling psalms; and he never failed to shed tears of emotion and groan audibly.

'After eating he made a practice of lying down for a little while, an hour, sometimes a little longer. Then he would read from the lives of the saints, and other books. In summer he would take a short walk in the monastery garden, or outside. At such times he had given me this order, which was always to be observed: "If you have something urgent for me, you must cough before approaching me, so that I can look around"; and I always did this. But one day it happened that as he was walking in the garden I coughed several times, wishing to approach him, and he was so deeply immersed in his thoughts that he heard nothing; he was on his knees, his face turned toward the East and his arms raised to the sky. I approached him, saying, "Your grace . . ." He was so startled that the sweat stood out on his forehead and he said to me: "Look, my heart is pounding like a bird's. But then I have already told you several times to cough before approaching me." He never set out on foot or in a carriage without his little psalter, which he always carried under his cassock. In the end he knew the whole psalter by heart. He also blessed me with this book. On the road he would always read the psalter aloud as he walked, sometimes chanting the verses aloud, and he would demonstrate or explain passages to me. Every day he would go to the Liturgy and sing in one of the choir stalls. He rarely sang without shedding tears. At the monastery of T., about midnight, he would go round the church, praying before each door, making genuflections, and shedding burning tears. I would sometimes listen, and would hear him say: "Glory to God above all the heavens," and he would begin to read the holy psalms. Before the west door he would pray more than half an hour, then he would return to his cell with rapid steps. There he would work hard, sometimes even splitting his own firewood. . . . One day he went for a walk behind the monastery and he told me, on returning to his cell: "I saw a dead tree in the forest which would make two cart-loads of firewood, maybe more. Bring the axe for chopping." We went into the forest and began chopping; he took off his cassock and began to work in his shirt. He would often say: "He who lives in idleness never stops sinning." He himself was never idle. In the morning before the Liturgy he would write his edifying books, which are still available and are read by a great many people seeking the salvation of their souls.

'Let me speak now of the simplicity and unselfishness of his life in the cell, for he owned only the barest necessities. As a bed he used a little rug stretched out on the floor and two cushions; he had no blankets, but covered himself with a sheepskin lined with cotton. He girded himself with a simple leather belt. He owned only one cloak, made of camel's hair. He wore big leather moccasins like those of a hunter, or peasant's shoes of plaited bark (*lapti*) which he put on only in the cell, saying, "How good these shoes are on the feet!" However, when he had to go to church or receive visitors he took off these shoes and put on the leather ones. His rosary was of the simplest style, of plaited thongs. He had neither trunk nor locker in which to put his things, only an old leather bag which he always carried with him on his trips, and in which he put his books and his comb. This was all his luxury. For three years he had a horse and a two-wheeled cart, given to him by the landowners B. After his rest he would go to the fields in the cart, sometimes also into the forest, where I always accompanied him. "Go and harness the cart," he would say to me, "and we'll go and mow a little grass for the 'old fellow' (which is what he called the horse, a very old one indeed) and drink a little water too." As we went along the road he never stopped talking; he would speak of the grass as an example of life, or he would explain some sentences of Holy Scripture. His words were always on the subject of eternity. Sometimes we went into the forest, and there he would mow the grass in the clearings himself, and would order me to put it in piles with my rake, saying: "Put it in the cart now, the 'old fellow' will need it to-night." Sometimes we would go to the spring, which is some ten versts from Zadonsk on the bank of the Don; and there we would drink the water. He loved this spring, for the water there was very pure . . .'

How simple this life is, how naïve and poetic in its simplicity! But this is not just a life that is peacefully sheltered. It has two pivots: the 'vigil' before the Divine Presence . . . and the service of one's neighbour. This man of prayer was at the same time a man who comforted and assisted his neighbours with a spontaneous and active concern.

'Now I shall speak of his works of charity and mercy,' continues Chebotarev. 'He fed orphans and the poor, he was charitable toward all those suffering poverty and distress—in short, he gave away all that he had, the pension he received from the State and also what the old Cossacks brought him. In Voronezh and Ostrogozhsk noblemen and rich merchants also sent him large sums of money. And not content with giving all his money to the poor, he gave away his private linen too, keeping only what he actually wore on his body. The bread which charitable merchants sent to him he gave to those who needed it, but this was not enough, and so he bought more. The poor and needy received shoes and clothing from him, and for this purpose he would buy furs, and suits of clothes, and linen. He even bought huts, horses and cows, which he then gave to the poor. But this was still not enough, and he began to contract debts. When he had given all away, he would ask me: "Go, I beg you, to Yelets, and borrow from this or that merchant. I will repay him as soon as I receive my pension, but now I have nothing. Here my poor brothers come looking for me and leave without having received comfort from me. It is painful to be able only to look at them." Sometimes it happened that he would refuse a poor person, and simply ask him who he was and where he came from. By the next day, however, this would be hurting him, and he would call me, saying: "Yesterday I replied to a poor man by turning him down; take this money, please, and give it to him. Perhaps we can comfort him in this way." All the poor had easy access to him. His humility was wonderful. He would speak to the old peasants, sitting with them, talking with them at length in a friendly way about the life of the village, and he would let them go in joy, having offered them whatever was necessary. Out of his own pennies he would help maintain the poor peasants who lived in the vicinity of the monastery, especially the widows and orphans, and would pay all their

I

personal taxes and duties to the State. He provided them with bread and clothing—in short, he helped them in all their needs. There were days when the poor who came were especially numerous and he had given away a great deal of money and other gifts. In the evening on those days he would be more gay and joyful than ever. But when only a few people came, or perhaps none, he was grieved. I can say this boldly, it was like Job's "the eye of the blind man and the leg of the paralytic." His door was always open to all the poor, the destitute, and the pilgrims who came to him. They would always find something to eat and drink with him, and a place to rest.

'He taught the little children of the village to go to church. How did this happen? When he came out of church they all ran after him. He entered his cell, and the children followed him there, made three deep bows, and cried out: "Glory to God!" And he asked them, "Where is our God?" They answered in a loud voice: "Our God is in heaven and on earth." "That's good, my children," he said then, and patted the head of each one, and gave each a kopek or piece of white bread and, in the summertime, an apple. Sometimes because of physical weakness he could not go to the Liturgy, and the children would go first to the church, but seeing that the bishop was not there they would go away. When I came back from the Liturgy he would ask me if the children were there. I answered: "Indeed they were, but when they saw that your grace was not there they went away." He would smile then gently: "That is all right. The poor come to the Liturgy to get bread and kopeks. Why haven't you brought them to me? I am very happy when they go to church."

'Likewise, the peasants who had to pass his house on the way to their work could always find an asylum of peace under his roof in the event that any one had fallen ill along the way. He himself took care of the comfort of the sick, even bringing them his own cushion and night cap; and he would give orders to make them more comfortable still. Two or three times a day he would pour their tea, would stay at their bedside for an hour or more, and would comfort and encourage them, carrying on with them friendly and intimate conversations. Some would be dying. He made himself responsible for them with the deepest and most

Christian compassion, and urged the sick to receive the Holy Communion. Those who were healed continued on their way, loaded down with gifts. In 1761 a great fire broke out in the city of Livny. The bishop did not fail to aid the victims. He sent the monk Mitrophan with money to be distributed. The next year a similar disaster fell upon the city of Yelets. Moved by compassion, the bishop manifested great charity. He went in person to Voronezh and Ostrogorzhsk to get money from his benefactors; to help build new houses for those made homeless by the fire; this was a tremendous help to them. He also visited those who lay in prison. At Yelets he visited the prison twice in person, comforting the prisoners, giving them helpful instruction and providing them with money and all sorts of other things. When a new prison was built at Zadonsk, with prisoners kept under very heavy guard, he was able to help support them too out of his own resources.'

His other servant, Ivan Efimov, has also left an account of Tikhon's life. 'At the time when the magistrate's court was located in a part of the Zadonsk monastery,' he writes, 'a prison for criminals was also established there. The bishop loved to go there at night to visit sick prisoners and give them gifts. On Easter, as he went through the prison, he exchanged the Paschal Kiss with all the prisoners. Again, in the city of Yelets, where he went from time to time at the request of the people, he would visit the prison and the home for the aged, and during this visit he would hide his episcopal rank under a simple vestment.'

'. . . at the very beginning of his stay at the monastery of Zadonsk he sold his silk garments, his light and warm cassocks, the double cloak of fox fur and the other garments of his office, also his eiderdown blanket and feather pillow and fine linen, for the sole purpose of giving the money to the poor. He even sold his handsome moire cloak, a gift of the bishop of Astrakhan—using the money he received to give to the widows and orphans.' [30]

Dostoevsky venerated the memory of Tikhon, and it is easy to see why he had this personality in mind when he was creating the *starets* Zossima.

•   •   •

[30] The journals of Chebotarev and Efimov have been published in the appendix to the complete works of St. Tikhon of Zadonsk, *Tvoreniya*, Moscow, 1889, Vol. IV.

This humility and simplicity was accompanied—as we have seen —by a *spiritual fervour* (Tikhon was praying alone in the garden with such concentrated ardour that he was literally startled when someone came near him) . . . and a *charity* having no bounds.

Let us say something more about this spiritual fervour. At the heights of religious experience in the lives of the saints spiritual tenderness (*umilenie*) can attain a great degree of purity and humble, sober illumination, it can become a permanent state, a sort of deep background or constitutive element nourishing the whole interior life. National differences lose their significance on these spiritual heights. And yet it is possible to speak of a piety and mysticism that is typical of the Eastern Church,[31] and to illustrate this piety and mystical experience with examples drawn from Russian religious life. This piety, especially at its best, is certainly not monopolized by or limited to the Russian or Greek or any other national element; on the other hand it is no less certain that this type of Orthodox piety has been decisive in the development of the religious ideal of the Russian soul.

On these heights, then, we often find a serene and luminous fervour, a glow of interior peace combined with 'spiritual tenderness,' often manifested in the 'gift of tears,' something which is discussed at length in the writings of the great masters of spirituality in the Eastern Church. We have the touching passages on this subject written by St. Isaac the Syrian: 'Here is the sign that you are approaching the borders of this mysterious country: when grace begins to open your eyes so that they see things in their essence, it is then that your eyes begin to flow with tears, which run in streams down your cheeks, and the conflict of the senses is subdued within.' [32] 'The heart becomes humble and little, like a child's, and when you begin to pray, the tears flow.' [33]

It is like coming into another spiritual country to read these writings. Thus, the monk Parthen, whom we already know, describes the remarkable figure of the 'schema-monk' John, a man

---

[31] This does not exclude close connections with the piety and mystical life of the Christian West; the root and foundation of both is the same: the living Christ.

[32] St. Isaac of Syria, *Homily 56*, from Russian trans. of 1858.

[33] ibid., *Homily 41*.

of very advanced age: 'The flesh of the *starets* John was so wasted away that only skin and bones remained. His face was radiant and full of joy, his eyes were always full of tears, and he could say nothing without tears. His words were kind, gentle and penetrating, so that he could move every one to tears. He had a lively gait, he ate very little, never any delicacies. He counselled patience especially, and obedience, temperance, humility and charity.' After refusing the insistent requests of Parthen for a long time, he finally consented to shed some light on the secret of his interior life. He had followed the path of 'interior silence,' and of 'pure,' continual and unceasing prayer. 'When I had spent many years in this way, then prayer began to deepen in my heart. Later, in the hermitage of Pokrov, the Lord visited me, thanks to the intercession of Father Platon. An inexpressible joy was born in my soul and interior prayer became possible. It fills me with such an inexpressible sweetness that I am unable to sleep. I sleep an hour or so, and then get up fresh and alert, as if I hadn't slept at all; even when asleep my heart is wakeful. And this prayer began to bear fruit. It is very true that the Kingdom of Heaven is within us. An inexpressible love for everybody was generated within me, and the gift of tears . . . when I wish, I can weep without stopping. And the Holy Scripture is now full of such sweetness for me, especially the Gospel and the Psalter, that I cannot read it enough. Each word fills me with wonder and makes me shed tears.'

We have in these words a glimpse of a life of extraordinary spiritual intensity, belonging already to another psychological order. Similar characteristics are scattered through the biographies which sketch the personality of this or that saint or just person, written by those who knew them well. Of course these are only brief indications, allusions to the riches hidden in the spiritual life. In the ancient *Life* of St. Cyril of Belo-ozero (*c.* 1400) we read, among other things, that 'he worked for nine years in the monastery kitchen, and acquired such a power of tenderness that he could not eat bread without tears. This holy man was so imbued with the love of God that when celebrating the Liturgy and during the reading of Holy Scripture he could not restrain tears of profound wonder and love.'

We find this same spiritual fervour in the life and writings of the great *starets* Paisy Velichkovsky. The letter to Mother Mary Protasevna, which we have already quoted in part, begins with a reference to the Saviour's words: 'I have come to bring fire upon the earth, and I desire that it be kindled!' (Luke 12 : 49). And the *starets* speaks at length, with amazing force, of 'this divine fire which the holy apostles received in their hearts,' and after them the holy martyrs, and all the other servants of God, a fire with which he himself was consumed.

Let us add a few words about that boundless charity, that great gentleness and kindness and fervent love for one's neighbour, that infinite compassion which is found on the summits of this spiritual life. Here we have the spirit of the first epistle of St. John. It is the spirit of the boundless condescension of the Son of God, by whom this love is inspired and from whom it comes, it is the 'humility of love' (*smirenie lyubovnoe*) about which Dostoevsky speaks ('the humility of love is an incredible power!'). In the writings of an old Russian saint of the twelfth century, Bishop Cyril of Turov, we find this prayer for one's enemies: 'Save, O Lord, and pardon, those who hate me and offend me, are full of enmity towards me and do evil against me and injure me, and also those who speak evil of me; let none of them suffer any evil as a result of my impurity, neither in this age nor in the age to come, but purify them after thy mercy, and cover them by thy grace.' [34]

The famous passage from the ascetical writings of St. Isaac of Syria about the compassionate heart 'inflamed with love for all creatures—for men, for birds, for beasts, for reptiles, for all that exists, even for the enemies of the truth'—a heart which prays to God unceasingly that they be delivered from their sufferings, preserved and purified [35]—these words have undoubtedly been echoed in the hearts of a number of Russian saints and ascetics. We know that the works of St. Isaac of Syria were well read in old Russia.[36]

[34] *Tvoreniya svyatogo Kirila episkopa Turovskago,* Kiev, 1880, p. xcvii.
[35] cf. Chap. II, p. 53.
[36] If we take into account the numerical ratio of manuscripts of the ascetical and mystical Fathers and doctors in the four principal libraries of old Muscovy (Trinity-St. Sergius, Solovki, Belo-ozero and Volokolamsk) the works of St. Isaac occupy second place (forty-five copies in the four libraries), second only to the *Spiritual Ladder* of St. John Climacus (eighty-two copies). St. Basil and St. Dionysius the Areopogite come next; cf. the remarkable and scholarly work of V. Ikonikov, *A Study of the Cultural Role of Byzantium in Russian History* (in Russian), Kiev, 1869, pp. 299–302, already quoted.

We have already referred to instances of this kindness and compassion in the life of St. Tikhon of Zadonsk and others.[37] Here are a few more examples.

The ancient biography of St. Denis of Glushitsa (1363–1437), written shortly after his death, speaks of his endless goodness. He would give to those who came to him with requests without trying to find out who they were, would give even to imposters. To his disciples, who wanted him to exercise greater reserve, he replied: 'Stop begging me to be deficient in mercy.' The same thing is said of Cornelius of Komel (1455–1537).[38] No one who asked help of him was sent away empty-handed. The resources of the monastery were always available to the needy. On one major feast day when a very large number of poor people gathered at the gates, all the monastery's money was given away. At this time it happened that the Grand Duke Vassily Ivanovich had sent twentyone rubles (a large sum for that time) to the monastery, and this too was distributed at once to the needy.[39]

This characteristic note of extreme humility combined with boundless charity, always ready to pardon and serve, has been captured by one of the greatest Russian writers in the wonderful figure of the peaceful old man Pambo (in *The Angel Sealed with a Seal* by Nicolas Leskov).

'So what more could I say?' the narrator tells us. 'If I were to insult him, he'd bless me; if I were to hit him, he'd bow down before me to the ground; a man with that kind of humility is invincible. What could he fear if he even asked to be condemned to hell? No, with his humility he'd chase all the demons out of hell, or convert them to God. They'd torment him, and he'd pray: "Torture me more cruelly, for I deserve it." No, no, Satan himself couldn't bear such humility. He'd wear out his two hands hitting him, he'd blunt all his claws and would end up acknowledging his own powerlessness before the Creator of such love, and would blush with shame before him.' Strange as it may seem, this is a quality taken from real life, it has really existed and is a special characteristic of Russian sanctity. We have here the type of a

---

[37] See preceding chapter.
[38] See preceding chapter, p. 100.
[39] cf. the work of Konoplev, *The Saints of the Vologda Country* (in Russian), pp. 50–9.

quite *supernatural gentleness.* Without meaning at all to monopolize it, we can say that this is an almost 'national' element in Russian piety.

More striking yet, perhaps, are the words of the old missionary Kiryak (in another of Leskov's stories: 'At the End of the World,' which is set in the far north-eastern part of Siberia). Carried away by the force of boundless love, full of trust in God, he contends with God before his death, catching hold of the hem of His garment, so to speak, and refusing to let go. 'I will not let go before you bless them all.' This is that same infinite boldness of love that we saw in Isaac of Syria.

This fervency of spirit—this immense love for men which sacrifices itself, multiplies good works, gives alms—the fervour of this constant pleading before God—all this was incarnated in the figure of the great man of prayer and active charity, the Archpriest John of Kronstadt (1829–1908).

. . .

On the heights of this life in grace we find, finally, a quiet, humble *jubilation,* or *illumination* of the spirit, despite all the earnestness of unceasing, courageous and indefatigable spiritual combat. The manliness of this struggle, the courage of this spiritual attitude is illumined and transfigured by the joyous experience of the nearness of the Lord. These qualities appear with special force in the life of the *starets* Seraphim of Sarov (1759–1833, canonized by the Russian Church in 1903), a life imbued with a supernatural radiance. 'Christ is risen, my joy!' he used to say by way of greeting to those who came to see him, all through the year and not just at Eastertide.

In this saint the *pneumatophoric* element, the penetration of the entire being by the Holy Spirit, is particularly prominent. He had attained the state of interior illumination, the inexpressible peace so full of measure and soberness which lies at the heart of the triumphant Paschal joy. Many witnesses describe him to us in this way. He himself says: 'Whoever admires the world cannot avoid being troubled. But he who despises the world is always in joy.' Particularly remarkable is his long conversation with the layman Motovilov, which the latter recorded carefully, and which was published posthumously in 1903. This was not merely a conversation, it was an ineffable experience, an illumination by the presence of the Holy Spirit. We approach a realm here where reverent silence should be preserved. 'The power of prayer is prodigious,' St. Seraphim said, 'and stronger than all that exists, for it is prayer that causes the Holy Spirit to descend . . .'

In conclusion I would like to refer to some elements in the life of the *starets* Makar of Optino (1788–1860), using extracts from a biography written by one of his disciples.[40]

'. . . One Maundy Thursday he was singing alone in the middle of the church the hymn "O my Lord, I behold Thy bridal chamber richly adorned," and as he sang it seemed that the words "I behold" had on his lips a literal and not merely figurative meaning, that the hymn was expressing what he was really seeing with the eyes of his soul. The old man's voice trembled with emotion, torrents of tears ran down his pale cheeks and those who heard him were stirred to the bottom of their hearts . . .'

'. . . His face was burning and luminous, like that of an angel of God. His expression was peaceful, his speech humble and without pretence. His spirit was constantly united with God in unceasing interior prayer, and by virtue of this untiring inner prayer his face shone with spiritual joy and radiated love for his neighbours. When he received the holy mysteries of Christ at the altar, it was always with the deepest emotion. His garments were of the humblest and simplest make. Up to his death the *starets* preserved his natural liveliness, which made him a very active person, always disposed to do good works. This liveliness always expressed itself in his actions and external gestures. He had an amazing memory. When someone came to make his confession to him, or had asked him for spiritual counsel, the *starets* would often remember all about him, all the main circumstances of his life. It often happened that an old woman would come to him for the second time, and would be greeted by him: "A very good day to you, Darya! Are the little ones all right? How is your daughter Trinushka? You married her off three years ago, if I'm not mistaken." And the poor woman, amazed and deeply moved that God's servant should have remembered her, would be at once consoled; her embarrassment

---

[40] cf. Archimandrite Leonid, *Skazanie o zhizni i podvigakh startsa Makarya,* Moscow, 1881.

and confusion passed, she would open her soul to him, telling him her cares and drawing comfort from his words.

'In all his qualities and external actions the *starets* lived in a regulated way: the "royal way," as the holy Fathers called it. He concealed his great temperance in his humility. He would eat all that was offered to him at the monastery table, but only very little, not more than a third of the normal serving.

'He was full of pity for animals. In winter he cared for the birds every day; he would spread out hemp seeds for them, on a little shelf he had attached outside his window. A flock of little titmice, linettes and woodpeckers used to enjoy the *starets'* favours. He used to watch that the bigger birds, like the jays, did not hurt the little ones. Since the jays tried to devour all the food meant for the other birds, he would put out grain in a little glass trough where the little titmice could easily get it.

'The *starets* would get up every day for morning prayer at the sound of the monastery bell, which rang about two o'clock in the morning. If, however, he was kept later than usual in the evening writing letters, or if he was indisposed, he would get up at three. He himself awakened his servants, knocking at their door so that they could say the rather long morning prayer with him. He would sing the hymns in honour of the Mother of God in a very loud voice. After the prayers he would send his servants away and remain alone before God. At six o'clock he would call the servants back in order to read with them the prayers for that time, and the Liturgy. Then he would drink one or two cups of tea and would turn to writing letters or reading. From this time on his cell was open to all who had need of his material or spiritual help. After a midday meal, he would close his door for half an hour, an hour, or more, and would then begin to receive the people who thronged to visit him . . .'

'. . . at times the *starets* would enter a state of spiritual joy, especially when he was meditating on the ineffable ways of God's Providence, or was conversing on this subject. Then he would often sing one of his favourite hymns, for example: "Come ye faithful, let us adore God the Three in One . . ." or one of the canticles which celebrate the inexplicable and unfathomable mystery of the Incarnation, and the most pure Mother of the

Emmanuel. Sometimes he would leave his cell and walk between the flower beds in the garden; he would go from one flower to another, plunged in admiration of the glory of the Creator.'

There is here a great spiritual synthesis, as there was in the life of St. Tikhon of Zadonsk. And in all these various qualities (in Tikhon's life too we hear a good deal about the inner struggle against temptation, melancholy and sadness) what stands out above all is this tranquillity, the peace of a transfiguration that has already begun.

These men were the guides of the Russian people on the path toward the summits of the life in Christ. Every nation has had guides such as these. Both the cultural and the spiritual life of the Russian people have been made fertile by their presence, their example and their teaching. No doubt the great mass of Russians— both at the top and the bottom of the social scale—were all too often unworthy of these saints. And yet, in spite of everything— and I am convinced of this—the saints continue to influence the history and destiny of this people.

CONCLUSION

INNUMERABLE reliable sources have recently demonstrated an unexpected flowering of the religious life in Soviet Russia. The Christian faith, long buried in the catacombs, took advantage of a more favourable atmosphere in the years immediately following the Second World War to spread with amazing vitality into various sections of the Russian people, even among members of the Communist Party and Komsomols (Alliance of Communist Young People). This has made the Communist leadership extremely uneasy, and measures taken against the Church and religion have become increasingly harsh since 1959. It is even possible to speak of a renewal of persecution (unbloody, but extremely painful nevertheless).

In the context of Soviet life any manifestation of religious feeling is extraordinary and yet they abound. Here are a few samples taken at random.

One of my friends, a professor of Slavic philology in one of the great universities of Western Europe, a Catholic who is a warm friend of the Orthodox Church, visited Moscow as a tourist at the end of 1958, and got to the Monastery of St. Sergius (Sergievo-Troitskaya Lavra), about forty miles north of Moscow. A long line of believers would form up in the evening in order to get into the Monastery Cathedral the following day. He himself was able to enter in the morning as a tourist, without difficulty, through a side door. He says that he has never attended a service as beautiful as this Liturgy at the Cathedral of the Dormition, in the St. Sergius Monastery. It lasted two and a half hours. The chants were magnificent. But what caught his attention especially was the congregation. Packed together in a church that was too small for the number present, they remained almost motionless throughout the service. But as they prayed tears ran down their faces, faces which shone with a fervour my friend had never seen before. Never had he seen people pray in this way. The majority were women, but there were also many men present, and not a few young people, some of them in uniform.

Scenes such as this, observed by many reliable witnesses, are

CONCLUSION

significant. They could be multiplied without end. Another characteristic feature here is the *courage* of the believers, often displayed especially among young people. We are familiar with the indignant articles in Soviet papers and magazines about the model student, the ornament of the university, the young scholar full of promise, suddenly discovered to have been at the same time one of the most active members of such and such a parish, where he took part, for example, in solemn processions around the church, carrying a sacred banner. The authorities, of course, did not suspect this 'double life'! Finally the denunciators and party spies found him out. The young man showed courage in his replies, and did not allow himself to be intimidated.[1] But his career was ended. Cases of this sort appear quite often in the Soviet press, and are always treated with the same righteous indignation : here are traitors to the cause of atheistic Communism, the hidden enemies, and what is more, 'persons of double life,' friends, comrades, the best of colleagues, and yet . . . they believe in God! They are traitors to the common cause! Have no mercy on them! Let them be consigned to the harshest kind of manual labour.[2] There are many cases of this sort . . .

Here is a young school teacher from the Kuibychev region (Samara), who writes that she is resigning from the ranks of the Komsomols because of her religious convictions. 'I am a Christian,' she said in the oral examination which followed her decision.[3] In the region of Tarnopol the majority of marriages are celebrated in the churches; the chief doctor of the Sidorovo Hospital (in the Gusyatin district), P. Melanenko, attends church often and even brings his child to receive Communion. The chief of rural police in a village of the same region, a member of the Communist Party, and his wife (a school teacher), have one whole wall of their house covered with icons.[4] In the same Communist review a denunciator describes in angry detail the great fervour he noticed

---

[1] This was, for example, the story of one Eugeny Bobkov, aged 20 years, student at the University of Moscow, in his third year in the Faculty of Law; cf. *Komsomolskaya Pravda*, April 12th, 1959.

[2] cf. for example *Komsomolskaya Pravda*, No. 76, 1959; ibid., February 14th, 1959; *Uchitelskaya Gazeta*, No. 40, 1959; *Kommunist Belorussii*, No. 1, 1959, etc.

[3] cf. the atheistic magazine *Nauka i religia*, No. 9, 1962.

[4] Article of V. Titov in the Soviet magazine *Krokodil*, No. 5, April 1st, 1962.

among the faithful at the famous Cathedral of the Dormition of the Virgin in Vladimir. Besides old men and many old women he saw a great number of young people, especially girls and young couples with babies.[5] Pilgrimages continue to be made even when the sanctuaries which attract the people have been demolished. Thus (according to a detailed and venomous article in the Soviet review *Oktyabr*) streams of pilgrims continue to make their way each year, on the 23rd of May, in the Kirov (Vyatka) region, to the village of Velikoretskoe, where as in the past there is an ancient and honoured icon of St. Nicolas. It is an irresistible popular movement. Prohibitions of local authorities are ineffectual.[6] Before the celebrated icon of the Virgin of Vladimir, which is at present in the Tredyakovsky Museum in Moscow, visitors often kneel and make the sign of the Cross, although this is expressly forbidden by a sign mounted near the icon.[7]

What is especially remarkable is the great number of Communions (especially at Liturgies celebrated early in the morning).

An external but eloquent sign of the fervour and number of believers are the very large sums of money taken up in the churches as offerings. It is truly said that it is *a believing people* who guard the Church, support her, maintain her, defend her. This makes it ever more difficult, in spite of all the government's efforts and all its hosility toward the Church, to return to the bloody persecutions of the '30s. In spite of all the malice and hostility of officialdom, and all the subterfuges, harassments and painful injuries inflicted upon the Church, *it is a believing people which must be reckoned with.*

I shall stop here. What is the end result of all these facts, as they appear on the background of contemporary Russian life? More servants of God of all ages, even among the youth! And the Christian faith, as so many examples show, is more and more alive and evident, not just as a pious and venerable tradition which restores links with the past, but as a far greater reality—*as a merciful and victorious Presence,* who reveals Himself to the heart and

[5] Article of K. Kostyukov in *Krokodil,* January 30th, 1962.
[6] Article of Mme. Alla Trubnikov in the Soviet magazine *Oktyabr,* 1962, No. 7 (quoted in the weekly *Posev* of September 10th, 1962).
[7] Report of a woman of Russian origin holding a professorship in a University of South Africa who had just visited Moscow (in 1962).

CONCLUSION

takes hold of the heart—and as the victory of the risen Christ, who reigns over and within those who believe in Him. It was just in this way that this message, this same Good News, once made its appearance in the world : as a *victorious Presence* which the powers of evil could not suffocate or destroy.